LIVING
WITH THE
MONKS

LIVING
WITH THE
MONKS

WHAT TURNING OFF MY PHONE TAUGHT ME
ABOUT HAPPINESS, GRATITUDE, AND FOCUS

JESSE
ITZLER

**CENTER
STREET**

New York Nashville

Center Street
Hachette Book Group
1290 Avenue of the Americas, New York, NY 10104
centerstreet.com
twitter.com/centerstreet

First Published in hardcover and as an ebook by Center Street in May 2018
First Trade Edition: October 2019

Center Street is a division of Hachette Book Group, Inc. The Center Street name and logo are trademarks of Hachette Book Group, Inc.

The publisher is not responsible for websites (or their content) that are not owned by the publisher.

The Hachette Speakers Bureau provides a wide range of authors for speaking events. To find out more, go to www.HachetteSpeakersBureau.com or call (866) 376-6591.

Library of Congress Cataloging-in-Publication Data has been applied for.

ISBNs: 978-1-4789-9343-8 (trade paperback), 978-1-4789-9341-4 (ebook)

Printed in the United States of America

LSC-C

10 9 8 7 6 5 4 3 2 1

This book is dedicated to my Grandma Sylvia and Grandma Fannie. Wish we could have one meal together.

Author's Note

I lived at a monastery and kept a detailed diary of my time there. The experience greatly impacted many areas of my life in a positive way. Some people who read my first book, *Living with a SEAL*, emailed me to say they wanted to do my next adventure with me. I would have loved to, but this was a personal journey. I had to do it alone. Plus, I don't expect anyone to leave their families, their daily lives, and go live with monks. And now you don't have to...I did it for you.

Removing yourself from the overstimulated world we live in can be difficult. So you must consider the withdrawal symptoms that may occur. Like any activity involving deep thought and introspection, some of the events in *Living with the Monks* may cause side effects like calmness, being present, and feeling super alive. And those side effects can become addictive, so all readers should take full responsibility when living a more vibrant life.

Some of the events in this book have been recalled from memory and in some cases may have been compressed to convey the substance of what occurred or was said. Some of the dialogue might not be verbatim, and I tried to keep the time sequence of my events in order. That said, it's possible things occurred either earlier or later in reality than they do in the story.

~~Roger that~~.

Namaste.

@The100MileMan

Contents

PART III · Ten Real-World Benefits

PART IV · The New Beginning

AFTERWORD · Post-Monastery Update to the Trade Edition

"He that is taught only by himself has a fool for a master."
—BEN JONSON

PART I
In the Beginning

Before and after.

Ding—beep—buzz

Ding—a text alert goes off.

I open my eyes. And with a glance, I check to make sure my wife, Sara, is still sleeping. Check.

It's still dark out, and the only illumination in our bedroom is my glowing phone.

Carefully I roll over to my right side and reach toward the nightstand to find it.

I need two tickets to the Hawks game tonight—the text says.

I got you—I text back.

As I sink back into bed I pull the covers over my head to eliminate the brightness of my phone. I don't want to wake Sara. I quickly refresh my email to see what's come in my inbox during the five hours I was sleeping—too many. I swipe it away. I check the time. It's 4:53 a.m. I have to get up because I have a workout appointment in seven minutes. SEAL, the man who kicked my ass and lived with my family for thirty-one days, is at my house. And the rule is: If SEAL is at my home, we're working out.

Two minutes later I check my email again—nothing new.

I swing my legs off the bed and quietly place both of my feet on the rug. My wife's still sleeping. I slip my phone into the pocket of my shorts and throw on the T-shirt that's balled up on the floor. I tiptoe out of our bedroom into the long hallway. All four of my children are fast asleep as I pass each of their bedrooms. When I reach the top of the stairs I hear another *ding*.

I manage to respond to the text as I walk down the steps and simultaneously fire off two emails before getting to the bottom of the stairs. I enter the living room and have one eye on my phone and the other on something SEAL is doing. He's fussing with the remote trying to turn the television off. He can't figure out which button to press. He's mad at the remote and looking at it like it's a Rubik's Cube.

I fire off one more email as he spots me.

It's 4:58 a.m. so I'm early.

"What the fuck is that?" SEAL asks, staring at my hand.

"This? Oh, it's a phone."

SEAL takes one more glance at the remote and now decides he's no longer pissed at the controller; he's pissed at me. I can tell he's annoyed—VERY annoyed. He's staring at me stone faced. He's not moving—like at all. For a second I think he's playing some wacked out version of "freeze tag" in his head. He's as still as a statue.

After about thirty seconds of just staring at me he snaps out of it.

It's like he was never still.

"Oh, it's a phone," he mimics like a three-year-old teasing his big brother. "Oh, it's a phone."

He inches closer to me—in my face. I'm not sure why he's so livid.

What did I do? It is in fact a phone. Right?

"You don't think I know what a phone is, Jesse? I USE

PHONES MOTHERFUCKER. I just used one yesterday. I know a phone when I see one. Oh, it's a phone," he says a third time as he bends down to lace up his running sneakers.

"I'm very sorry," I say, trying to make peace. "I just thought—"

"I KNOW WHAT A PHONE IS, JESSE."

I try to craft an apology in my head. I'm not sure why, but I feel like I owe him one.

"Sorry," I say again. "I just thought you asked me what's in my han—"

"Jesse, are you committed?"

I'm confused. I'm not sure where he's going with this.

"LET ME SAVE YOU SOME TIME MOTHER-FUCKER," he says. "You're NOT."

Huh?

"I'm sorry," comes out of my mouth a third time.

"You and that damn phone," he says. "You need to clear your mind, Jesse. To be committed."

He's so angry that one could mistake his "committed" to mean sending me off to a mental institution. But I'm pretty sure he's talking about making a commitment—to myself. And maybe he's right. I do need to unplug. But unplugging is only half of a fix—I need to plug into something else—something bigger than myself; a 180, to get uncomfortable again, a self-imposed time-out and find a growth opportunity. SEAL helped me get physically fit and sharpen my mental toughness. But now I need something that'll help quiet my mind and create a new kind of edge.

I look back, and SEAL is already holding the front door open for me.

"Let's go for a run," SEAL says.

I'm not sure what happened, but it's like someone flipped a switch and he's fine again—not mad. It's like I never even had a phone. As I follow him out the door I fight an urge to check my email one last time.

A Few Days Later...

I click on a link that a friend sent me—a picture of Thich Nhat Hanh, the Vietnamese Zen Buddhist supermonk, pops up on my computer screen. The photo is, well, I don't know, likeable. But it's not so much *how* he looks, which is a pleasant face with protruding ears and a balding head, but the *way* he looks. It appears like he's operating on a higher plane. This is what I'm searching for—I need to figure out how to spend a few weeks in his shadow.

I want to live on his monastery.

My wife always tells me I'm too impulsive, that I don't think things through before taking action, and it gets me in over my head sometimes. Maybe, but I like to go with my gut. And my gut is telling me that he's my guy. I start reading the article.

It turns out the holy monk (I'm not exactly sure how to pronounce his name: Tic-Not-Han? Maybe? We'll call him "Thich" for short) lives on the Plum Village Mindfulness Practice Center in the Dordogne region in the south of France. He's a master of spirituality and mindfulness—he trains people to become fully present, which sounds fantastic EXCEPT you have to commit to the place for five years, freeze all of your bank accounts, and you're not allowed to see your family during the first two years of "monkism."

I may be able to get over the five-year commitment, but not seeing my family is a nonstarter.

Okay, so his isn't the shadow I'll be walking in anytime soon.

Although living with Thich might have been a tad aggressive, I'm not ready to give up my spiritual quest. My life is abundant, but sometimes I feel overwhelmed. On top of electronic and social media accessibility 24/7, there are my four kids and their schedules, to-do lists, businesses appointments, charity events, workouts, and running routines. And somehow amid all of that I have to find time for my loving relationship with my wife. I shouldn't say "have to"—I *want to*.

But above all, I want to learn something new. I start imagining how much I could accomplish if I blocked out all of the noise in my head, prioritized my time, and learned to be truly present in the moment. I need a Plan B.

I pick up my phone and speed-dial my literary agent, Lisa Leshne.

"Hi, Jesse," Lisa says after one ring.

I hear wind whipping against her phone. She's probably walking her dog, Luna, somewhere in Riverside Park on the Upper West Side of Manhattan, because just as she says hello to me, I hear her tell someone that Luna's a rescue dog.

"I want to live on a monastery," I say.

"Um, okay," she responds. "But don't you mean *at* a monastery?"

"Either way. I just want to go live with monks."

"Any particular reason?"

"I did the physical part. Now I want to explore the spiritual side. I want better focus. Stronger mind-set."

"Aren't there podcasts for that?"

"Perhaps, but I need to immerse myself—just like I did with SEAL."

And that's when the idea hits her. She tells me to hold and then patches me in with the editor for my book *Living with a SEAL*, Kate Hartson. When Kate answers, Lisa tells her I'm on the line.

"I hope you're ready for this one. Jesse wants to go live with a monk," Lisa says. "Or multiple monks. And I believe you know some monks who might fit the bill!"

There's nothing but silence.

Kate must think it's a terrible idea, but my mind is made up. I want to do this. I'm waiting to hear her reaction, but it doesn't matter what she says. I don't need her to sign a permission slip. I'm locked in.

"I actually know of a monastery where you can go," Kate finally says.

"You do? Would they freeze my assets, and tell me I can't see my family for two years?"

"Excuse me?"

"Are they in the south of France?"

"Well, no. The monastery is in upstate New York."

"Upstate New York? That sounds perfect. Can I go for a couple of weeks?"

"I'm pretty sure they'd be happy to have you."

"Okay, book it. Two weeks or so, for some personal development. Some *me* time."

"Don't you want to know more about them?" Kate asks.

"Are they monks?"

"Well, yes."

"That's all I need to know."

If my wife was with me, and she's not, she'd shake her head and say something like: See what I mean about not thinking things through?

"Okay," Kate says in a tone that sounds like she thinks I'm a little chemically imbalanced. "But they're called the monks of New Skete, just in case you get lost."

An hour later...

I pick up my phone and dial my wife.

"Sweetie, can we talk for a second?"

"Sure, my love," she says. "What's up?"

"I'mgoingtoliveonamonastery."

I'm hoping it was fast—fast enough so she only half hears me, except my wife doesn't have "half hearing." She has whole hearing. She heard me perfectly clear.

"A monastery? As in MONKS?"

"Yes. As in silence, meditation, and monks."

I can tell from the long pause that Sara is processing the information. That's what Sara does—she's a processor. She thinks things through before making a decision. I, on the other hand, am a reactor. I hear the word "challenge" and immediately react with, "I'm in!"

And in this case, Sara taking her time is justified. Some guys need an excuse to go to a bachelor party in South Beach or a hall pass for a weekend in Vegas. But I'm trying to go to a monastery, which is a lot to process. So before she responds, I follow it up with a kicker to help my cause.

"And it's going to make our marriage even stronger, sweetie."

"Stronger?" Sara asks. Then she repeats the word again, with more curiosity: "STRONGER? Explain that one to me."

"Well, I think it'll help me appreciate our time together. Be more present. Stuff like that."

"Jesse, this sounds like an excuse to go run a marathon somewhere with your friends."

"No, I'm serious. I'm planning on going next month."

"Then, love, have you lost your marbles? Because there are plenty of other solutions to make a marriage stronger, like maybe we should just go for more walks together."

She has a point. But this isn't really about making our marriage stronger.

I need a different angle—quick.

A few years ago I realized I was watching an awful lot of football. College games on Saturday and the NFL on Sunday, Monday, and Thursday were on my viewing schedule. It was excessive. And while I did love watching the games, I calculated that if I kept on that pace and lived to be eighty-two years old, I'd spend (waste) another 36,000 hours of my life watching football. Think about that—watching other people play a sport. It was a wake-up call. So I immediately unplugged the TV and went cold turkey. And right after I made the decision I told Sara that I had just freed up 36,000 hours of my life to use as I saw fit. That's 1,500 days...four years. So then Sara asked me what I was going to do with all of that newfound free time.

"Some of those hours are for you," I said with a flirtatious smile. "Some are for personal adventures."

And right now feels like a good time to pull out the adventure card! It's worth a shot.

"I'm using some of the 36,000 hours I freed up, sweetie."

"Really, darling?"

Okay now, don't let Sara's blonde, bubbly charm fool you. She built Spanx, one of the most popular women's undergarment companies in the world, and she did it entirely on her own with $5,000 of savings and no investors. So she can smell when there's something fishy going on.

"So it's going to make our marriage better, huh?"

"MUCH."

"You know, sweetie? You're so full of shit, but you're darn cute. If you want to go live at a monastery, then you should go and enjoy yourself, Mr. Monk."

Okay then—it's set. **One of my favorite business rules is: DON'T OVERSELL—when you get the order, shut up and leave.**

So I respond with, "I love you, dear," and immediately hang up.

The next couple of weeks are business as usual. Sara is supportive but leery of my plan or lack of planning. She wishes I'd do more research and preparing. But when I'm ready to do something, I don't let anything slow me down. Ready, fire, aim.

Soon I'm counting days instead of weeks and then hours instead of days. It's almost go time. The night before I'm set to leave for the monastery, I craft a social media blast. It's partly a heads-up to tell people I'll be off the grid for a while and also a request for suggestions for a book or two that I should bring. Moments after I hit send, my phone starts to sound like a Las Vegas casino—dings, beeps, and buzzes. It doesn't stop.

Along with commenting on favorite books—*How to Be a No-Limit Person, Mindful Parenting, Man's Search for Meaning*—I get suggestions for blogs on meditation, spiritual guides to follow on Twitter, podcast recommendations, and must-watch documentaries about happiness, mindfulness, and soul-searching.

Everyone has a favorite. The comments keep coming in: ding—beep—buzz.

The responses are passionate and from people who have found a helpful nugget to make their daily lives a little bit better. They're eager to share—of my 1,000 career Instagram posts it's the most commented one of all time. As I look at my phone, I realize I've hit a nerve. The search for living a more meaningful life is a viral topic. And yet, it seems, at least the way my life unfolds on a daily basis, that we don't have time for anything that isn't announced with a ping.

And here's the thing: Every day, information, news, and entertainment bombard us. It comes at us from all angles, like we're under attack. We are living in complete information overload. Meanwhile, we're losing, or have lost, our most significant asset—the ability to think for ourselves. At every turn, we're told what to do, where to go, and what to like. Twitter, Instagram, and Facebook make decisions for us. Alexa, Siri, and Google Home tell us how, when, and where for everything else.

But we weren't wired this way; it's more of a learned

trait. All of those pings over time have trained us to read and respond immediately. As soon as an email hits our inbox we feel the need to respond right back. It's gotten to a point that it controls our time. And yet, I've always been a guy who relies heavily on his gut. Or at least I used to be. When your combined score on the SATs is 900, you either have a good gut or you don't go very far in life. And my instincts have served me well, but as my wife always tells me, **the only way to be in tune with your gut is to be alone—thinking. I've found that if you lose your "gut feel" you lose one of your greatest secret weapons. In fact, in virtually all areas of life—instinct is critical.** When it's firing on all cylinders, the force is always with you. And for me, it's always guided my decisions on friends, work, and life adventures.

As I scroll through the thousands of responses to my post, I start to get energized.

I know I'm on the right path. The path to the monastery!

I'm in Big Trouble

"He will win who, prepared himself, waits to take the enemy unprepared."

—SUN TZU

November 2017—New York City— Eight Months after the Monastery

How do you say *I'm fucked* in a Zen-like way?

Well, I better figure it out—quick.

I'm not ready for my meeting so I'm rooting for traffic as I zip up Sixth Avenue in the back of a cab. If there's enough of it then I'll be so late they'll have to cancel the appointment. I'm not looking forward to what's about to happen. But unfortunately every traffic light instantly turns green as we approach it—we keep moving.

It's been eight months since I left the monastery, and today I'm supposed to deliver a manuscript to my publisher about my monk experience. And I've got nothing. I should say practically nothing. I do have my journal with me, notes I jotted down each night in the tiny room (monks call it a cell) I lived in for fifteen days, but that's it. The taxi pulls over to the side of the street. I pay the cabbie and step onto the midtown Manhattan sidewalk.

A public relations mogul once told me that the key to crisis management is to get all of the bad stuff out in the open and on the table right away. So maybe that's what I should do in my meeting. I should come clean with my editor right out of the gate: *I'm screwed, Kate; I have nothing. Oh, and good morning.*

I'm standing on the corner of Sixth Avenue and Fifty-Fourth Street when the light changes; the sea of business people who surround me take off like it's an Olympic sprint. I, on the other hand, am in no hurry to cross the crosswalk to get to Hachette Book Group, my publisher. Perhaps I should lead with a positive and sugarcoat the crisis rule: *Good morning, Kate, you look great, did you get a haircut? Oh, and by the way, I'm screwed.*

I push the glass revolving doors and enter into the wide-open lobby. There are two people in a heated argument over a food delivery in the building foyer, but no one seems to notice them. Instead, they just swipe their cards on the electronic turnstile and rush to an elevator without buttons. Everyone seems so busy.

I start to make my way over to the front desk.

"Jesse," I hear behind me. "Jesse, over here."

I turn to see Kate. She's smiling and holding two steaming grande Starbucks lattes. I go over and give her a hello hug, careful to not spill the lattes of course. She was the editor on my first book, which exceeded her expectations. And it's the sole reason she bought the monk book idea. But the window to lead with my bad news has already opened and shut. We walk over to the elevator bank. I'll just tell her about the book situation when we sit down in the conference room.

The Hachette main desk is on the fourth floor. Kate's office is on the fifth. We walk up a staircase to an open room that's filled with editors quietly editing and assistant editors quietly assisting. The cubicles are full of smart-looking people. There's something very Zen about it.

I follow Kate as we snake our way to a windowless conference room.

When Kate slides the door shut it's like we're hermetically sealed. She turns to face me.

"I can't wait to see what you have, Jesse," she says, smiling.

I manufacture a smile and stare back. Kate's still smiling. She's excited to see the manuscript.

"It was a little more difficult than I thought," I say in a voice that sounds like I'm nine.

Her smile begins to fade...it's like a half-smile...and there it goes—it's gone.

"The monks don't really do much," I say. "They're monks, after all."

"Well, surely you have something," she says.

"Surely," I say. "One hundred and fifty blank pages of me being silent."

Now her smile is a distant memory. I wait for her to say something.

"What happened?"

There's a certain freedom in being totally screwed. When you're totally screwed, things can't get any more screwed up.

And in that moment, totally screwed, I find the confidence that only comes with being screwed. I push back on the rolling chair; get real comfortable.

"Let me start at the beginning," I say. "Like all great spiritual journeys, this one starts on a mountaintop."

The Visibility from Mount Washington

"Everyone wants to live on top of the mountain, but all the happiness and growth occurs while you're climbing it."

—ANDY ROONEY

January 2017

I have to start somewhere, and well, this seems like the perfect spot. It was about two months before I arrived at New Skete. And I wasn't thinking about monks or monasteries; no, I was focused on the challenge in front of me—the mountain.

My friend Kevin the cop had mentioned climbing Mount Washington the previous summer in passing, like someone asking if you wanted to grab lunch next week. Kevin's a police officer in Suffolk County, and at first glance, you'd never guess he's capable of Van Damme-ing an entire bar full of bad guys. He isn't all that tall, but he's beastly strong and fit. But when you get up real close and look deep into his eyes, you can see the extra "screw loose" gene. And yet, Kevin is also one of the most optimistic people I know. He's positive all of the time; unless of course he's kicking your ass, but even then, he's positively kicking your ass.

When he casually threw out the invitation for a new adventure we were at my house in Connecticut. Every year I hold a race called "Hell on the Hill." It's a steep grassy incline that you attempt to run up and down a hundred times, but sometimes it includes paramedics. It's hard. Someone who's REALLY in shape can do it in two hours and forty minutes. Kevin knocked it out in one hour and forty-two minutes. He won the race and beat me by close to an hour. I was bent over trying to catch my breath when he threw the offer out. I asked him how high Mount Washington was between breaths, he said 4.5 miles in a way that made it sound like a walk through the mall.

Once I caught my breath I asked if it was okay to bring some friends along. He said sure. So I invited my trainer, Marq Brown, who played linebacker at Auburn and for the New York Jets. He said yes because he's always down for a challenge. And then I extended invitations to my buddies Adam Hyncik, a finance guy, and Nick Morris who started Health Warrior energy bars, and they both immediately said yes.

I'd never climbed a mountain before so I had no idea what we were getting into, and I knew nothing about Mount Washington. So when Marq asked me where it was, I said, "Vermont, I think."

It turns out the mountain is in New Hampshire. I should have just said New England.

Seeing as it was Kevin's idea, I should have known the climb wasn't going to be easy. The first hint of how hard it might be came a few days before we were supposed to leave.

I received a couple of emails from him. The first one included a packing list: ice axe, crampons (which are shoes with spikes in them), and multiple layers of Arctic clothing. An ice axe? I had none of the equipment, and we were climbing the mountain in two days. What the...?

The second email had one word in the subject line: SURVIVAL. The first thought that came to me was, you mean there's a chance I won't? I immediately hit print and put it in in my suitcase. I mean, any email with the subject line SURVIVAL is one that I want to keep.

After the second email, I figured I better get a look at what I was getting into. I pulled up the mountain's Wikipedia page on my laptop. How can I explain this? Well, one of the toughest mountains to climb in the United States is Denali in Alaska. And Mount Washington in the winter makes Denali look like a bunny slope. Okay, maybe that's an exaggeration, but the winds at the summit of Mount Washington have been recorded at 265 miles an hour! Mount Washington has one of the highest death rate among climbers of any mountain in the United States. Temperatures can sink to minus 35 on any given day. The climb is a shitstorm of pelting snow and frigid air that blasts you in all four directions and that's why the mountain earned the title "The World's Worst Weather." Yeah, I said to myself, a walk through the mall.

I quickly headed over to REI with Marq to pick up gear for both of us, as we had nothing. One of the items Kevin strongly suggested was a "minus forty" sleeping bag to keep us warm in anything above minus 40 degrees—the plan, he said, was to spend one night sleeping outside on the mountain, and then summit the next day. Sleep outside? On the mountain? And with temperatures that get to minus 35, we need a minus 40 sleeping bag to protect us—that doesn't seem like a big margin for error. When I spotted a salesperson in the store, I asked for the minus forty bags.

"We're in Atlanta," the sales guy said.

"Right."

"We don't have a lot of calls for those here."

"Do you have two negative twenties?" I asked. "Or a ten and two fives?"

"Are you serious?"

I was serious: If I could wrap myself in two of them it might work. Right? We needed something. I raised my eyebrows a bit to try to get a real response from him. But instead, he delivered one of those pained, try to not be a jerk-off kind of smiles that certain salespeople have perfected. We were striking out.

Instead, Marq and I purchased the warmest gloves they had and bolted from the store otherwise empty-handed. At home, I fired up Amazon Prime and ordered the rest of the gear we needed with next-day delivery. And that night we had a scheduled conference call with the group to go over everything with Kevin. It was kind of like our pregame pep talk.

Kevin took us through point by point what we could expect from the mountain.

His voice was calm, which started worrying me a bit.

"What's the greatest risk we face?" I asked right after he wrapped up the game plan.

"Someone breaks their leg, and we have to carry them down the mountain," he said. "If that happens we're real shit fucked. They can't land a helicopter up there."

What?

"But it's cool; I'll carry the injured party down and come back for the rest of yous."

I'm not sure if "yous" is a word or not, but I let it go.

"What if *yous* break your leg?" I asked. "The rest of us don't know the way down."

The line was silent for a moment.

"Good point," Kevin said, finally. "I'll bring Jack."

Jack, as it turned out, was a survival expert, something every mountain climb should have. After the call I decided I should try to get a good night's rest, but I could barely sleep—tossing, turning, and thinking—thinking, tossing, and turning. When my morning alarm finally rang, I'd felt like I only had an hour of sleep.

And then at 6:00 p.m. the next day Marq and I landed at Boston's Logan International Airport. The mountain was about 170 miles from Logan, which took us about four hours on the snow-glazed roads. Eventually we pulled into the ice-covered driveway.

The house we rented looked precisely how you think a ski chalet should—wood everything, stone fireplace, and bunk beds. When we were finally inside, some seven hours after we left Atlanta, I could feel the excitement brewing like an old-school Mr. Coffee machine. Kevin and Jack were already there. With his weathered skin and military gray haircut, Jack looked like a cross between a drill instructor and the Marlboro Man. He even talked with a raspy voice. He was the kind of guy you'd follow into battle, or up a mountain.

When I unpacked my boots, they still had the tissue paper in them. I felt like the kid who shows up at hockey camp with brand-new equipment and then skates on his ankles. I quickly pulled out the tissue paper and shoved it in my pocket.

In the kitchen of the house, we had an impromptu huddle. Kevin went over the particulars of the mountain again: the height, visibility, or lack thereof, and how long he figured it'd take us to climb, which, he said, was about an hour for each mile, which meant it should take us close to five hours to reach the summit. When I asked what was the most dangerous thing that could happen besides breaking a leg, Jack answered.

"People have been known to walk off the mountain because they couldn't see the edge," he said, sounding like Quint talking about sharks in the movie *Jaws*.

"You mean they just step off?"

"The quick way down."

He added that we'd be all right if we stayed close, and walked single file with Kevin up front and him in the rear. People have stepped off the mountain??? It was a visual I didn't need planted in my head.

Fifteen minutes later, I was clomping around on the wood floors with my new boots and, five minutes after that, my legs were so tired it was like the boots were made out of cinder blocks. They were also as stiff as ski boots; it felt like they were cutting off my circulation at the ankles when I leaned forward. How the hell was I was going to climb a mountain in them? Next I put on my brand new backpack and clomped around. It wasn't going well. If this had been a slasher flick, the audience would have pointed to me and said, "Yup, that dude right there? He's going to die first."

Kevin explained that packing your backpack is one of the most important things someone climbing a mountain can do. It's paramount to survival. It can mean life or death when you're up there at zero degrees with zero visibility. Showing us, Kevin precisely placed all of my items into the pack: insulation, winter coat, three pairs of gloves, water, food, and goggles. All the essentials are up at the top and easy to access. It's kind of like elevator science—first in, last out; last in, first out. The sleeping bag goes on the bottom, then your heaviest jacket, heaviest layer, lighter jacket, light layer, hat. Goggles and gloves are on top with extra ski hats. Your insulation roller (you need something to put under the sleeping bag when you sleep so you don't freeze, as you lose the most heat through the ground) is tied to the bottom of the backpack. Three bottles of water are put in insulation sleeves that dangle from the side of the pack. And you fill them three-quarters of the way, so they freeze slower. Food is in the outside pockets. Then you also have an ice axe attached to your backpack. Fully loaded, the pack weighs fifty-seven pounds.

Fifty-seven pounds while wearing stiff cinderblock boots. No problem!

It was the eve of my next big adventure, so I blasted it all over Facebook, Twitter, and Instagram that I was at Mount Washington. They say that **_one of the best ways to accomplish a goal is to have an accountability partner._** What better way to do that than putting it out on social media. Immediately the responses started coming in: "I didn't know you're a climber!" and "A cold weather guy!" and "You're on top of the world!"

And with each response I could feel the pressure rising.

The next morning we got up at 0500. After breakfast at a local diner, we drove forty-five minutes to the mountain. The first thing I saw when we arrived was a sign that said: AVA-LANCHE DANGER. Avalanches? Nobody told me about avalanches. Neither Kevin nor Jack reacted to the sign. It was as if it was as common as a SLOW—Children Playing Sign.

We parked the car, unpacked, and prepared for our climb.

And then we headed over to the mountain.

"People slide off the mountain. One thing you have to learn before we start in case one of *yous* guys fall and start to slide is how to stop the fall," Kevin said, as he showed us how to stop ourselves with an ice axe on a small hill before the climb.

So, to recap, in climbing Mount Washington you can break a leg, walk off the mountain, the winds have blown at almost 300 miles per hour, visibility is less than zero, you need to use an ice axe to stop *yous* from sliding off the mountain, and *yous* could freeze to death. Other than that, there was really nothing to it. As I watched the demonstration I thought to myself, yup, Sara might have been right, I tend to jump into things without thinking about the consequences.

Aim, fire, ready?

I guess I started to get a little case of cold feet (even in my stiff mountain boots)!

"Hey Kevin," I said privately. "I heard something about tour guides. Do we have one?"

"No," he said.

"Any reason?"

"It's a fucking mountain, Jesse," he said. "It goes up."

"But…"

"You lived with a Navy SEAL," he said. "And if we get lost, we'll just use the Force."

"Well, at least we have Jack," I said. "He's kind of like a tour guide."

"No, Jesse, Jack's a human ambulance—that's it."

Even though it was zero degrees when we were about to climb, I wore only a long-sleeve Patagonia performance T-shirt to start. The cardinal rule of hiking in the winter is NO COTTON. When cotton gets wet, it ceases to insulate the body because all of the air pockets in the fabric fill up with water. And when you're lugging a fifty-seven-pound pack—even in zero degrees—you begin to sweat quickly. Sweat is the enemy because if you sweat and cool off, you'll get hyperthermia. At least that's what Kevin and Jack told me. And I believed them. They said one of the keys to surviving the outdoors in the cold elements is to control your body temp as best you can. And as you go higher in altitude, you begin to layer up. A mile up you put on a long-sleeve shirt, above the tree line, a light jacket, and at the top—your Arctic jacket. It was go time.

We started to climb.

Higher…

And higher…

Our first goal was to get to where we would camp for the night, which was about 2.2 miles up the mountain, and we arrived there a few hours later. The "camp" area consisted of a series of wood platforms with roofs. No walls—they were fully exposed. Luckily, we found one that had snow bank walls creating an igloo effect to block the wind. The plan now was to bunk down for the night and get an early jump on the climb the next morning.

The view of the other mountains was incredible, but it was still too snowy to see the top of our peak. And it was only 2:00 p.m. So we had nineteen hours before our next go time. Nineteen hours. Nineteen Atlanta hours go by like a flash. Nineteen New York City hours feel like nineteen minutes. But here at base camp, it seemed like a very long time.

Immediately Jack pulled out a small propane tank and started a fire. Later he made a dinner for us of oatmeal and pasta. The sun went down at 4:30 p.m., and we ate by flashlight. At about 7:00, we went out for a hike. There was nothing to see in the pitch darkness, but it was good to have something to do.

We bumped into another hiker while we were out, the only other human we saw in hours. The guy had a Grizzly Adams beard and wintery weathered skin, and he was eating an apple with NO GLOVES. No gloves? I had two pairs of gloves on AND glove warmers, and my fingertips were still frozen. It looked like this guy lived on top of the mountain and hadn't been anywhere else in his life—ever. Adam asked him if he'd ever summited the mountain. Adam, you fucking moron, I thought, of course this guy has summited the mountain. That's like asking Aquaman if he swims.

"Thirty-seven times," the guy said.

By the time we got back to camp the conversation was played out and so, with no cell phone service, radio, internet connection, there was nothing to do. There were absolutely no distractions. I started to get tired. It was either the thin air or clomping around in the boots that did me in. We all zipped into our sleeping bags. Kevin boiled water to put it in our water bottles and instructed us to put them in our sleeping bags to warm them up. It worked. I felt like a frozen burrito in the microwave.

I looked at my phone. It was 8:03 p.m. I could feel and see my breath. In and out, in and out, in and out; I kept watching and feeling my breath. I stayed like that for what seemed like hours. And then I closed my eyes again and just focused on the warmth inside my sleeping bag. I remained still, just passing the hours in my frigid surroundings. There was no sensation of time, and when I finally opened my eyes, I thought it was a day later.

I looked at my watch; it was 8:25 p.m.

Only twenty-two minutes had passed?

That was impossible. Twenty-two minutes?

A thought came to me, the first of several that would lead me to a monastery. This one was as clear as the mountain air, and it was delivered in a voice that was like a whisper in my ear: My relationship with time is out of balance.

When I'm in my routine—time flies. When I'm not in my routine—time slows.

It was a feeling I wanted to bottle up and save.

At 6:35 a.m. I was up and anxious to start. It was cold as FUCK. I threw on my jacket, slipped on my concrete boots, and walked ten yards away from "camp" in the thick powder to urinate. When I got back I ducked right into my sleeping bag to get warm; everyone was already up and chatting.

We made a safety plan. If we didn't get to the summit by 1:00 p.m., then no matter where we were on the mountain we had to turn around. After that time, it would get too dark and too dangerous. We all agreed—it was a pact.

We started to get ready to roll. On went my boots, thermals, and backpack. Jack had told me yesterday to hold my breath when I put on my goggles, or they'd fog up and it'd be 100 percent impossible to defog them. I took a huge breath like a sixth-grader jumping into the deep end of the pool. And then I quickly put my goggles on to test the method. It worked. It was time to climb.

9:15 a.m.

We came upon a tree on which was tacked an avalanche report. It instructed us to go back about a mile to take a different approach. GREAT...Jack and Kevin seemed to take this information in stride. But I had an image in my head of body surfing a massive wave of snow—unsuccessfully. We did an about-face and headed back from where we'd come.

10:30 a.m.

Eventually we started to hike higher; most of the snow had been blown off the mountain, but there were spots where it was up to the top of our boots and walking through it was like walking in a wading pool filled with glue, only up at a forty-five-degree angle. The climb was so steep we had to hold on to trees or roots; otherwise we'd fall. Now I understood how people slid off the mountain. The new plan called for us to reach the summit by 1:30 p.m., which would still give us enough time to get back down before sunset.

But we agreed that 1:30 was the absolute new cutoff time.

"We'll make good time until we get above the tree line," Kevin said. "Then it'll get hairy."

"What do you mean...hairy?"

"You'll find out," he said.

Noon

We took a trail called Lion's Head, "the winter route." This is where things get real according to Jack. From there, we'd either try to make it to the summit or turn around to go home. And that's when I learned there's a HUGE difference between above the tree line and below the tree line. We were no longer protected from the elements. When we reached the top of Lion's Head, the gusts had to be at least forty miles an hour. It was like someone turned a snow machine on in my face. The wind blew a fine powder, making it hard to see my hand in front of me. Instantly it was like we were in a giant snow globe that had just been picked up by a rambunctious eight-year-old—the snow was shaking at us from all angles.

"GRRO TUR LEFFFF," Kevin shouted.

"WHAT?"

"GRRO TUR LEFFFF."

"WHAT?"

"GO TO YOUR LEFT."

I moved to my left.

At this point, to communicate, everyone had to yell. And still, we could barely hear each other with the wind and snow whipping around. Kevin pulled out orange sticks from his pack to mark our trail so we'd know our way back as we inched higher. But the problem was I couldn't see the sticks a few steps after I passed one. I looked back, and it was like they'd instantly disappear.

"We need four hours of daylight to get back to base camp," Jack yelled over a gust of wind. "At the rate we're going we'll never reach the summit in time."

We all sort of stopped and huddled and the snowy wind kept whipping around.

It was decision time. Kevin looked slightly concerned.

"Guys," I yelled. "I got four kids and I'm friggin' scared. We made a pact."

No one debated that. Plus, these were those important instincts I mentioned earlier that we all need to rely on.

"We're only a quarter mile from the top," Kevin said, almost like he was trying to convince himself to keep going, but we collectively decided to turn around.

It was only when we returned safely on the flat earth that the disappointment set in. Still, the whole experience had left me with a sense of exhilaration. When you climb something so high and so dangerous, you feel like you're the first person on the planet to do it. But it was more than just the challenge. On the mountain, I could actually feel time—sense it. I could touch it and hold it. The higher we climbed, the more real it felt. People often tell me time is precious. But they don't really know. They only think it's precious when it's gone, or it's slipping by. **On the mountain, time felt precious because of the way you experienced it; there were moments, not minutes.**

Four Days Later

I was sitting in bed with Sara and still not over the disappointment of not completing the challenge of the mountain. My email was filled with friends reminding me that I didn't make it.

"Must be tough to get that far and not finish," one of them read.

"I failed," I said to my wife, putting down my phone.

"No, you didn't," she said. "That's crazy talk."

"No, I failed. I took my friends and we didn't make it. I need to go back."

"That's a wonderful idea, sweetie. Plan a weekend next winter, get a tour guide, you numbskull, and properly break in your boots."

"Next winter?" I said. "Next winter? NO WAY.... I'm going back on Saturday."

"Saturday?"

"Yes, THIS Saturday. I have no guarantee I'll be here to do it NEXT winter. I have no idea if I'll be healthy enough NEXT winter. I'm going back this weekend."

The mountain reminded me how important time is. **Putting things off can often lead to regret.** Acting now, even if the timing isn't perfect or everything isn't figured out, has always been the way I operate. It's often the difference between failure and incredible accomplishment. **You can't outsmart time, but you can learn to maximize it.** I was going back on Saturday.

That Saturday

After a lot of processing by Sara, I got a hall pass, but this time it was for only twenty-four hours. There was no overnight. The plan was to climb up to the summit, get back down before dark, and then fly home. We estimated the climb would be about ten hours round-trip. Kevin reviewed the safety procedures, and we started on our journey up the mountain around 7:00 a.m.

As we climbed higher and higher and higher, it felt like we were walking on the moon. There was a freezing mix of pelting snow, fierce wind, and icy ice. And it was layered with a healthy amount of fear.

And then, five hours later, the same crew from last week, plus a local guide, stood on top of the summit of Mount Washington hugging in celebration! There are 7 billion people on the face of the earth, and yet it felt like we were the sole survivors—the last of the human race, alone and frozen in time. **As we made our way down the mountain I was reminded of a quote I love by Haruki Murakami:**

"And once the storm is over, you won't remember how you made it through, how you managed to survive. You won't even be sure, in fact, whether the storm is really over. But one thing is certain. When you come out of the storm you won't be the same person who walked in."

The trek up Mt. Washington.

In that frigid isolation, another of those guiding thoughts came to me: I needed this feeling permanently in my life or at least a way to access it when needed. And I didn't know it at the time, but it was the beginning of my journey to the monastery.

Getting ready!

Here I Come

"Everything changes, nothing remains without change."
— BUDDHA

March 2017—The Night before the Monastery

I'm not a selfie guy—not even close. Don't get me wrong; I'm as vain as the next guy. But how many times can you look at your own picture? I just don't get it. But here I was, standing in my living room, staring at my hair, about to take a selfie.

I checked myself in the mirror and pulled my hair back as tight as it could go to see what it was going to look like. Hmmm...I wasn't so sure about this. I turned my head to the left and got a profile view, and it wasn't much better. I grabbed my phone and flipped the camera so I could get a nice tight shot of just my head. Snap—snap. And then I took my finger and tried to block out where my hair was, but it still wasn't doing the trick. I needed something else.

I went to the App store and searched for: "Make me bald."

I scrolled through the numerous options and decided on: Baldify—Go Bald $0.99. Secretly, I was hoping I'd look so ridiculous I wouldn't do it, but the clock was ticking. Jessica, my wife's hairstylist, was on her way over. She comes to our house to cut Sara's hair about once a month, and I usually piggyback a trim off it. I called her earlier in the day for an emergency appointment. Finally the app downloaded.

Just as I clicked it open, I heard the front door open and shut.

"Heeeellllo, honey, I'm home," Sara said. "And so is Jessica."

While my wife kissed our four lovely children hello, Jessica transformed our bathroom into a pop-up salon. I put the phone in my pocket and sat down in the chair. I'd just wasted $0.99 on the app. Jessica wrapped me in a black smock, and I looked in the mirror. I have curly blond hair that's a bit unruly. It's been my trademark since I was a kid. It's like my version of Madonna's beauty mark, Fonzi's jacket, or Nelly's Band-Aid back in the day. It's my thing. I've always worn a headband or ski hat with my blond locks leaking out. But though the decision was a drastic one, I'd made up my mind. I was going bald!

"Sara," I yelled, "It's go time."

I needed my wife to watch; this was an emotional moment, and I wanted her support.

Sara walked into the bathroom with a pretzel rod hanging from her mouth like a cigar.

"Tell me this again, sweetie," she said. "Why in the world are you shaving your head?"

"Because it's required."

"Required?"

"I'm going to a monastery, silly."

"This is ridiculous. Ridiculous. Don't you think you're being a bit...extreme, Jesse?"

"Extreme? Not at all. I have to do it. No hair is basic monastery 101. Going with a mop of hair would be disrespectful."

Sara snapped off a bite of her pretzel.

"I can't believe I signed up for this," she said. "I really can't believe I signed up for this."

There must have been an echo in the room. But it's a known fact in our marriage that when Sara tells me about something that bothers her she says it twice, sort of like Jimmy Two Times in *Goodfellas*, except Sara isn't an Italian mobster. She's my primary.

"I know, honey," I said. "And that's why I love you."

"Fire it up, Jessica," she said with another chomp of her pretzel. "Shave it all off."

Jessica plugged in the razor and flipped it on. It sounded like a swarm of angry bees. I closed my eyes when the electric buzzzzzzz went next to my ear. I felt the cold metal teeth touch the skin at the base of my skull. Jessica slowly slid the electric razor up to the top of my head. I looked down to see my blond locks bounce off the smock and hit the ground in a little hairy pile. I closed my eyes again, and when I opened them, I looked more like Walter White from *Breaking Bad* than a monk in the movie *Gandhi*.

Sara and I spent the next hour staring at my shaved head—not really, but I kept taking a peek in the mirror while we got the kids ready for bed. We have four; all of them are under the age of seven, so organization and efficiency are keys to success. We've devised a kind of human carwash.

Sara takes our two three-year-old boys in the bath and helps them. She washes, they splash. Then she passes them over the tub to me, where I towel dry them, apply their Pull-Ups, and put on their pj's. Meanwhile, my oldest son, Lazer, age seven, gets in the tub next. The grand finale is our daughter, who is fifteen months old, and the whole process takes about twenty minutes.

And then from there, it's story time with mommy and tuck-in time with daddy.

The next morning I was in full-on hustle mode, completing the final preparations for my trip. I'd written a list of all the scheduled activities for the kids to give to Sara (even though it's on her calendar) and put together "to do's" and "where are they's" for her: get banana chips for the kids, lock the doors at night, where the soccer cleats are. I was transcribing them onto Post-its and sticking them to the refrigerator door when I looked over and noticed Sara peering into my open suitcase. It was like she was eyeing a penny she dropped into a wishing well. My bag contained fruits and veggies—lots and lots of fruits and veggies. I had dozens of bananas, twenty-six apples, three bags of organic carrots, thirty oranges, a box of spinach, and three sticks of celery— for garnish. I packed it myself.

For twenty-seven years, I have only eaten fruit until noon. The fast explanation is that most digestion requires a tremendous amount of energy. That's why if you eat a big meal you often get tired afterward. So if we streamline our digestion and use less energy during the process, it frees up more energy for everything else. Fruit, if eaten correctly, digests super efficiently. So I wanted to ensure I'd have enough of a supply at the monastery. Who knows what monks eat? In fact I know nothing about monks outside of what I've seen in the movies, and my only recollection is that they are small, spiritual, quiet, and oozing with wisdom. You never see a monk eat in a movie—weird, right?

"I'm assuming there are clothes in here somewhere," Sara half said/half asked.

"Yes, honey."

"Did you pack a robe, Mahatma?"

"Ha. I actually thought about it, but they'll probably give me one, right?"

"I was kidding."

"I'm not. I'm going full Dalai Lama: robe, sandals, the whole bit."

"Sandals?"

"Absolutely."

"Isn't this place in Vermont?"

"Upstate New York."

"It's the middle of March, Jesse. They probably have four feet of snow."

"Snow is a nonissue. It's 72 and sunny. Mind over matter. Plus, I'll probably be meditating half of the day anyway."

"Meditating? That's a funny one. Um, how do I say this politely, Jess? You can't sit still for half a minute, let alone half a day! Just last week at your friend's wedding ceremony you kept tapping Orlando's shoulder and then you'd pretend to be asleep when he turned around. You're the least likely to go to a monastery."

"I love you," I said with a kiss. "But I've got to go. I'll call you when I land."

My Uber driver dropped me off right next to the Delta gate. I slung my pack over my back and wheeled my suitcase of produce across the crosswalk. I had plenty of time. The flight didn't leave for an hour or so. The electric sliding doors opened as I walked into the Atlanta airport without breaking stride. The check-in gate was right in front of me. There was no one in line, so I rolled right up to the agent. She greeted me with a sweet Georgia, how-can-I-help-you smile.

After I got my boarding pass, I took a stroll. I wasn't shopping, just killing time. I popped in and out of a couple of stores, living in my own world when I heard: "Last call for flight 261 to Albany."

Showtime.

I race-walked to the boarding gate and was the last one on the plane.

I was in seat 2A. The guy in seat 2B ordered a Bloody Mary. He kind of looked like an unprepared high school substitute teacher; something about him screamed, "I'm in transition!" Maybe it was his ill-fitting suit, or perhaps it was the comb-over. Regardless, when I looked over at him again, he smiled a toothy grin.

The flight attendant brought him a can of V8 and two little vodka bottles.

I'm not usually into the seatmate small talk that occurs on a plane, especially with some guy firing back Bloody Marys at 10:00 a.m., but sometimes you just get sucked in.

"Albany," 2B said as he cracked the first vodka bottle. "Not some of God's best work."

I tried to give him a genuine laugh, but it was hard. It came to me that I should pull out my journal and start

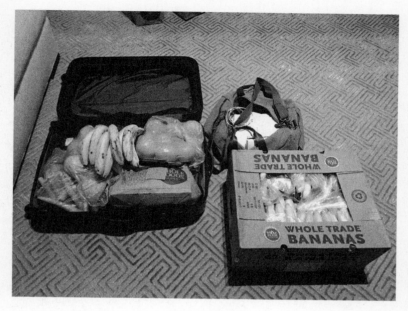

All packed up!

writing. Most people are smart enough to pick up on that hint. So I started writing; I wasn't sure where to begin, so I wrote down anything—anything that came to mind. After a while I felt like I was starting to catch a groove. That was until...

"What do you do?" 2B asked, slurping his filled-to-the-rim plastic cup.

"I'm an entrepreneur," I said. "But I'm focused on living life for a living."

"Nice...and weird," 2B said. "What's in Albany for you?"

"Well, to that point," I said, "I'm going to live at a monastery."

"Like on purpose?"

The first landmark.

No Sleep Till New Skete

"The only true wisdom is in knowing
you know nothing."
—SOCRATES

My longtime friend Turney Duff offered to pick me up at the Albany airport when he heard I was coming to New York. And as I walked out of the terminal, I saw him standing in the parking lot. He was leaned up against his Honda Civic hybrid smoking a cigarette. I walked toward him. He let out a puff of smoke and looked directly at the top of my head.

"You sick?"

"No," I said. "I told you. I'm going to live at a monastery."

He nodded like he'd just put it all together.

"Last time I shaved my head I was in rehab."

"It kind of feels like that's where I'm headed," I said.

"Why are you doing this anyway?"

"I want to unlock the how. The how to be a better version of me. You know, learn how to have better habits, better routines, and a better mind-set. Then I can share the secrets."

"You had to shave your head for that?"

"Well, at a minimum it's going to be good to step away from my phone and get off social media. I mean, do you think Thomas Edison would have ever invented electricity if he was on Instagram all day?"

"I'm pretty sure Ben Franklin is the electricity guy. And he didn't invent it—he discovered it, you jackass."

"Same thing. And thank you for picking me up."

"You're welcome. And I figure if you get all wise and shit at the monastery, well then, some of that might rub off on me for being involved. Right? Like the transitive property."

"Turney, I love you, but with all due respect you're just driving me there. That's not really being involved."

"Then get the hell out of my car," he said with a smile.

Before throwing my bags into his trunk, I checked on my fruits and vegetables. SHOOT. All of the bananas had gone brown. Damn it. It must have been too cold in the baggage compartment of the plane.

"This is going to seriously mess up my morning ritual," I said.

"You're worried about messing up your ritual? You're going to live with monks," he said. "Rituals are the least of your issues."

"You think it's going to be hard?"

"Harder than you think. It's not like running a marathon," he said. "Where you're done in a few hours and you get to relax on your couch. There's no escape from the monastery."

"You're probably right, but what the fuck do you know about running marathons?"

He ignored my question as I continued to check on my fruit. I discovered two bananas left that were still yellow with brown spots; all of the others had turned rotten. I offered a good one to Turney.

"I don't do fruit," he said. "Unless it's in a Pop-Tart."

We hopped in. Okay, there's no polite way to say this—his car was disgusting. It smelled like an ashtray and there were empty Coke bottles all over the floor and what looked like some kind of animal fur on the seats.

"Do you have pets?"

"I don't," he said. "Why?"

"No reason."

It was about an hour drive to New Skete from the airport, and we were about a half hour into the trip when I noticed the amount of snow on the ground. The snow banks on both sides of the road made it feel like we were traveling in a bobsled. And the names of the towns and streets we passed seemed misspelled or random, maybe both. Actually that wasn't fair of me. In 1980 I got knocked out of the sixth-grade spelling bee in the first round. And I'm talking the first-first round, not in front of the school, nope—I didn't even make it out of the classroom. My word was "bicycle." I spelled it how it sounded: "bisickle."

But then we passed a sign for Hoosic River, Requate Road, Marpe Road, and then Clum Road. It was like they forgot a letter in each of the names or maybe I'm still a terrible speller. Since Turney and I were way past the point of small talk, I passed the time by Googling the street names. "Hoosic" is an Algonquin Indian word; "Requate" is someone's last name; "Marpe" is Hebrew, I think; and "Clum" meant "quiet" in Old English. But there was neither rhyme nor reason to them. I hoped it wasn't a sign of things to come.

After a while, Turney asked if I was hungry, which I suddenly was. We pulled over at Benson's Restaurant. It looked like it may have been a house at one time. The parking lot was half full, and all of the vehicles were pickup trucks

(mostly with hunting stickers on the bumpers), and virtually all of them had snowplows attached. The snow crunched
underneath our boots as we crossed the parking lot.

"I'm thinking they don't make smoothies here."

"Um, I'm guessing they probably serve live bison here."

I was right—no smoothies. But it turned out they did have
a salad on the menu. I ordered two and asked the waitress
to bring the second round when I finished the first. Turney
ordered mozzarella sticks, potato skins, a cheeseburger extra-
rare, and French fries. It's amazing he's not four hundred
pounds—he's not even half that. Oh and a Diet Coke, too.

"I have a high resting metabolism," he explained.

I made a mental note to try to be more of a positive influence on his health when I got back. Eventually, our waitress
brought the first round of food. As she set down our plates I
decided it was a good time to ask her if she knew anything
about the monastery. I mean, we were pretty close to it so . . .

"Hello ma'am, we're heading up to New Skete," I said.

"Are you a dog lover?"

What a strange question to my question, I thought. The
waitress smiled.

"No, I'm going to the monastery."

"They're not cheap, but they're adorable when they're pups."

"I'm sorry," I said. "I'm actually going to the monas—"

But she had already disappeared back into the kitchen
before I could finish my sentence. I looked over at Turney to
see if he was as confused as I was, but he was having an inti-
mate moment with his fried food.

Back in the parking lot when we finished, I told Turney I

needed to make a few phone calls before we hit the road. I'd
heard there was no cell service at the monastery, so I figured
I should get all my last calls in before I went radio silent. Just
as I was about to dial my mom, I got an incoming buzz. I
checked the screen, and it was my friend Dorit. She's a yoga
instructor in New York City. She's a good friend, but we hardly
ever talk on the phone. I hoped everything was okay.

"Hello—"

"ThankgodIcaughtyou," she blurted. "I saw Facebook.
You're going to live at a monastery?"

"Not forever," I said. "What's up?"

"But it's going to be silent, right?"

"I don't know," I said. "I think so. How've you been?"

"Whatever you do, don't take the vow of silence."

She was making the word "vow" sound like a batch of Jim
Jones's Kool-Aid.

"Wait, why?"

"My friend. He went on a silent retreat. Seven days.
When they finally told him he could speak, he couldn't stop,
like, ever. He just kept talking and talking and talking."

"Huh?"

"He hasn't stopped talking since," she said. "It got so bad
he was institutionalized."

"Come on?"

"I'm not kidding. I've been up to visit him. He just sits in
a chair talking to a wall."

"Um, this isn't the conversation I'd like to have right
before I get there."

"I'm sorry, but I'm dead serious. If they ask you to be
silent, just say no."

The road that leads from the grid to off the grid.

Off the Grid

*"Be where you are, otherwise you will miss
your life."*
—BUDDHA

A worrisome feeling sank to the bottom of my two-servings-of-salad-filled stomach.

I was heading for the big slowdown.

"You okay?" Turney asked as we started driving again.

"Not really. Dorit said after taking a vow of silence some guy ended up in a funny farm."

"Why?"

"Because he couldn't stop talking."

"About what?"

"I don't know. And I hope I don't find out."

Turney told me we were about five miles from the monastery. I turned and looked back out the window. The Honda's wheels spun on some ice and then caught the dry country road. We were in a part of New York State not a lot of outsiders know about. People often associate New York with skyscrapers and the sidewalk outside of the *Today Show*. But upstate is rural, real rural. I mean like a secret kind of rural that the locals don't want you knowing about. We rode through a town that looked like the word "neighbor" still meant something. It was quiet and quaint and had character.

I rolled down the window, and a blast of cold air slapped me in the face. The rolling tires on the pavement had a sort of hypnotic buzz to them. I noticed a shift in the atmosphere. It felt different. I looked over at Turney to see if he noticed it too.

"It feels very monkish up here," I said. "You feel it?"

"It feels fucking insane up here, that's how it feels."

We passed snow-covered farmland, with old barns and claptrap houses that looked like they were about ready to fall. I was starting to get lost in the sights when I realized there were a few more texts and emails I should fire off. I tapped out a text to Sara and hit send, but the little circle in the upper corner of my phone just spun uncontrollably. I'd lost cell service already. I was officially off the grid.

We went through another little town, and the road started to climb. Except for the snow-covered evergreens, the other trees were bare—spindly branches that were kind of eerie. We were in the middle of nowhere. And I mean nowhere. Like if they hired SEAL to find us, he'd struggle to locate our coordinates. Finally, we saw a wood sign that read: NEW SKETE.

As Turney's car climbed higher and higher, the road seemed to become narrower and more treacherous. Even though the sun was out, and a minute ago it made the snow gleam, now it was dark under the soaring pine trees. His car continued to climb the road like it was on a chain lift for a rollercoaster. And after a few minutes up the mountain, I finally spotted something other than nature.

It was a large green building on the right, and it looked

industrial, a large Quonset hut type of thing. And then another fifty yards up a similar type building was visible. We drove higher. And at the top of the road a thicket of birch trees opened up, and I saw the monastery, which was a one-story building made out of barn board painted a rusty red. It looked like a mountain ski lodge except for all the crosses on the roof. Wait, what? Crosses? And not only crosses, but the kind with the big gold, onion-shaped bulbs on the bottom like you see in St. Petersburg, and not the St. Petersburg in Florida.

"Holy shit," I said.

"Dude, don't pair the word 'shit' with the word 'holy,'" Turney responded. "That's not going to work up here."

"This is not..."

"What you expected?"

I should have done a little more research into this place. But I didn't want to have any preconceived notions of what I was getting into. So I was a little blindsided by the whole Christian thing. I grew up in a mostly Jewish town on Long Island. I mean, going Buddhist is one thing, but Christian? I guess I knew there were Christian monks; I just didn't think I was going to be one of them.

I took in the landscape. The monastery was cut right out of the side of a mountain surrounded by full pine and other trees that were winter bare. Sara was right. The snow was about four feet deep and it muffled all sound; the place was completely soundless. It was so quiet when we got out of the car I could practically hear my heart beat. When you're always surrounded by noise the absence of it is a little unnerving.

"You hear that?" Turney said.

"What?"

"It sounds like . . . nothing."

He and I walked across the snow-covered parking lot until we got to the shoveled walkway. I set my steel wheeling bag down and pulled. The noise the wheels made rolling on the pavement sounded like a bowling ball headed down the alley. It echoed—echoed—echoed—echoed.

"Pick it up," Turney said. "It's too loud. You're going to piss off the monks."

So I did.

The main building of the monastery was made out of wood planks painted red, with a pitched roof that was covered with a foot of snow. In front of the building sat a wooden bell tower that was two stories high. Then there was another building to our right and up a walkway with several more crosses on the roof. And then I spotted the yellow door.

The only prior communication I had with the monastery was one email—that's it. And thankfully the subject line wasn't SURVIVAL. I pulled out the instructions I received in that correspondence. It said to find the yellow door upon arrival and just open it. The information specifically said, "DO NOT RING THE BELL."

As we approached the entryway there was a sign on the door next to the bell.

"DO NOT RING THE BELL."

Okay, I got it. They didn't want the bell rung. The bell equaled noise.

I could tell Turney was tempted to ring and run, but he resisted.

I opened the door and quietly tiptoed into the entryway. It was so damn quiet.

Immediately it felt like I'd just stuck my nose into an old unopened library book. If monasteries have a smell, this was it—a musky-earthy odor that was somewhere between sleepaway camp and a funeral parlor. There were old photos on the wall of men in group shots. Some of the images were black-and-white, and in them, the young faces were topped with dark hair. But in other pictures, some in color, those same faces were older and the hair had gone white.

Turney followed me as we walked down a dark hallway looking for someone to help me. But there wasn't even a hint of anyone in the building. It was library quiet. We kept walking. And then the hall opened up to a dining room. Long wooden tables were placed in a rectangle, with wooden chairs all around. I peeked my head around the doorway and saw a guy sitting at the far end. He was alone just sitting there like a librarian. He looked helpful. Or maybe he was my only choice; regardless, I slowly approached.

On the floor next to him lay a giant German shepherd that barely raised his eyes.

"You must be Jesse," the man said as he stood.

He was the authentic version of what young hipsters are trying to look like. He had a scraggly beard, thinning brown hair, glasses, and navy blue sweatshirt. I told him I was Jesse and then introduced Turney. We all shook hands.

"Did you find the place okay?"

"Yes, thanks to GPS," I said.

"Good, good. We're a little remote, but we like it that way."

"I'm supposed to speak with Brother Christopher," I said.

"Well, you are."

"You're Brother Christopher?"

"You sound surprised."

"I'm sorry. You're just not what I expected."

"Ahhh expectation. That often leads to disappointment. Well, what did you expect, my friend?"

I ran my hand over the stubble on my skull.

"Oh," he said, looking at my nearly smooth dome. "We all have hair here. Well, except for the brothers that lost their hair by the Lord's will."

The Lord's will? The Lord blessed me with hair and I voluntarily shaved it off.

Turney looked at me and shrugged. I had a feeling like I was lost or maybe in the wrong classroom on the first day of school. I was hoping for the full Buddhist monk experience, and instead, I got a gentle guy who looked like he worked at a farmer's market every Saturday and Sunday with a big dog by his side.

Just then, Brother Christopher's German shepherd came to life to sniff me out.

"Her name is Raisa."

After getting a quick whiff, she darted to my rotten banana–filled suitcase. She went nuts wagging her tail and scratching at my luggage trying to open it up.

"Raisa, down," he said.

The dog immediately retreated and then sat.

"Whoa. That was amazing. Is the dog for security?" I asked.

"In a way," he laughed. "Here take a seat."

We all sat at the dining table and started to chat.

It turned out Brother Christopher knew a lot more about me than I did about him—he'd read *Living with a SEAL.* SEAL one-liners from my book like *"Google me, mother-fucker"* flooded into my consciousness. What had Brother Christopher thought when he was reading it? Did he read it after he'd already agreed to let me stay at the monastery? Was he already regretting the invitation? Or was he going to suddenly stand up and scream, "Tranquility test, motherfucker"?

Of course not.

Although I barely knew him, he had a soothing, soft way that put me immediately at ease.

"I enjoyed the read very much," he said.

"Thank you. I really appreciate that."

"It was visceral," Brother Christopher added. "And reading it was like watching a movie. SEAL has a lot of the same qualities as monks."

What? Do these monks do 2,500 push-ups a day, run on broken bones, and sleep in oxygen-deprivation tents?

I started to question if Brother Christopher had really read the book.

"You should invite SEAL to the monastery."

"Wouldn't that be something."

"Do you still speak with him?"

"I do."

"Do you still have adventures with him?"

As a matter of fact . . . I was in Los Angeles six months ago with SEAL trying to get a TV deal. I thought (still do) the story was perfect for a sitcom, like *Fresh Prince of Bel-Air* meets *Rambo*. How could they say no, or so I thought?

So I told Brother Christopher this story but gave him the PG-13 version of it.

SEAL and I traveled separately to L.A. and met the first morning at my hotel. In the Uber on the way to Century City West, I explained to SEAL the significance of our meetings and tried to put it in language that'd really appeal to him: "My mission is to get a TV deal before we leave Los Angeles. And we've got forty-eight hours to get it done."

SEAL slowly turned his head my way. I was familiar with his expression.

"YOU THINK THIS IS A MISSION MOTHER-FUCKER?" he said. "A mission? This isn't a mission, Jesse. You have no idea what a mission is. At best this is a want, and a want and a mission aren't even in the same atmosphere. A mission? What the fuck do you know about a mission???"

He's right—I haven't even seen any of the *Mission: Impossible* movies.

But I thought there was a little latitude with that word. I knew better than to disagree. I saw the driver checking us out in the rearview mirror, but he quickly looked away when SEAL spotted him. There was a long pause, and the car filled with silence, the uncomfortable kind.

The driver started driving faster. And SEAL looked even more agitated then he was moments before. It was like his agitation was growing. With every block we drove he seemed more pissed off. Finally he started fidgeting with the seat belt, and it defused him like a fidget spinner.

"If I'm being generous, I'd say today is your goal," he eventually added. "BUT IT'S NOT A MISSION."

Roger that! I made a mental note to be careful using the word "mission" with SEAL.

In some circles, SEAL is known as the toughest man on the planet. But the main thing you need to know is he has a zero-tolerance policy for bullshit. It's one of the first lessons I learned from him. Regardless, we both agreed we were in Los Angeles for a reason. And I knew without SEAL there was no book—and without a book there was no television deal.

Our driver dropped us off in front of the valet at Fox Studios. We were there to meet Jeff, our Jerry Maguire. I had talked Jeff up big-time to SEAL and hoped he'd live up to the billing. And when Jeff strolled up, he was wearing a bold pinstripe suit that stood out starkly in the California sun. His smile was just as bright. The only thing he was missing was a catchy theme song while he walked toward us in slow motion. Though he wasn't your typical Hollywood agent, he looked the part. Jeff was about ten feet away when SEAL turned around to our group.

"Who the hell is this clown?"

"That's our agent."

"Well, why is our motherfucking agent wearing perfume?"

I prayed Jeff wouldn't use the word "mission." And thankfully he didn't.

We had two meetings lined up that day, ABC and Fox. The plan was for the hired writer and our motherfucking agent to pitch the storyline and we'd chime in as we saw fit.

For the Fox meeting we all convened in a giant conference room. It was like the beginning of the movie *The Warriors*, when all of the gangs in the City meet up in the Bronx for a special meeting. There was a Fox gang, a CAA (Creative Artists Agency) gang, a production company gang, and a *Living with a SEAL* gang. But instead of everyone wearing their "colors," they were dressed up in business attire, except me and SEAL—we were casual. The meeting was so big it felt like the assistants of the assistants were in there taking notes.

I was shocked to see the average age across the table from me. It seemed like all of the decision makers were younger than thirty—male and female. And boy could they talk. Ninety minutes of talking—and talking—and talking—and talking. Everyone was pitching everyone.

But the vibe wasn't working and I looked over at SEAL to see if he was picking up on the same thing. And I think he was about eighty-nine minutes ahead of me. He stayed laser focused on the pitch document in front of him. He hadn't said a single word the entire meeting. As I said before he has no tolerance for bullshit—and I could tell he was DONE. But they kept talking.

The meeting was close to wrapping—it had to be—right?

And then one of the younger female executives sort of head-nodded SEAL with a smile.

"Hey you," she said with a light laugh. "Are you going to talk?"

SEAL stood up. The room went silent.

"I ONLY talk when I have something intelligent to say. I don't just talk to hear myself talk."

BOOM—that was the most intelligent thing said all meeting.

The meeting was over. And on to ABC where things didn't go much better.

The next day at CBS I told Jeff to let SEAL and me pitch the story. I thought we could tell it much better as *we are* the story. It's like I always tell young entrepreneurs, **"YOU ARE THE BUSINESS PLAN."**

And that went much better; we ended up with a deal at CBS.

"But the deal fell through," I said. "So we're still out there shopping it."

And then Brother Christopher stood up and smiled. His dog did the same without the smile.

"Well, why don't we get you started."

My cell.

The Tour

"When the student is ready, the teacher will appear."
—BUDDHIST PROVERB

Brother Christopher led the way. There wasn't a whole lot
to see. The kitchen was the size of what you might find at a
small summer camp; there was a little gift shop with books,
a meeting room, and a small reading room. The three of
us, Turney, the dog, and me dragging my banana-filled suitcase, followed our monk guide. On the way, he gave us a
short history of the monks of New Skete. The name comes
from the Greek word Skete, which means a small, monastic
order of monks. The first Sketes were in Egypt thousands
of years ago. The New Skete monks started out as part of a
Roman Catholic Order of Friars, but then a dozen or so of
them asked for permission to branch off to find something a
little more intense, more monastic.

They first moved to a hunting lodge in northwestern
Pennsylvania. Then, in 1967, they bought 500 acres at $50
per acre on Two Top Mountain near the village of Cam-
bridge, New York. Once there, with the help of local people,
they built the entire monastery by hand.

"Monks have always been self-supporting in the most

authentic sense," Brother Christopher told us as we walked down the wood-paneled hallway. "The founders of our monastery did everything and anything they could to support themselves including farming, carpentry, and animal husbandry."

I saw Turney stifle a laugh. He must have had images of lonely shepherds playing in his mind.

"Of course, all that changed when we went to the dogs."

Went to the dogs? I didn't get it. The monastery seemed to be doing fine.

Brother Christopher stopped and opened a door to a small, sparse bedroom.

"You'll be sleeping here," he said. "I hope you find it comfortable."

My monastery room was about eight feet long by six feet wide, about the size of a big closet. No television, no computer, no anything. In fact, all it had was a single bed with a faded red plaid bedspread, a thin gray blanket. Next to it was an old night table with a lamp. That was it—nothing on the walls—nothing on the floor, nothing to read.

The bathroom was tiny with a shower that looked like it was built for someone four foot seven, and there was a half-used bar of soap in the tray. It reminded me of the bathroom you'd find in a rented RV. The toilet bowl sat unusually low as well. I immediately realized I wasn't in Kansas anymore. This was real. I was in for something transformational—different. I was way out of my comfort zone and about to be tested. *I always tell myself I can't get growth unless I take action.* Looking around my small empty room I recognized I was in action mode.

And then Brother Christopher looked right into my soul with his piercing blue eyes. He leaned in real close. He was two inches from my face and I felt like he was luring me into some kind of standing trance. It was like he just went into a phone booth as a hipster from New York City and came out a monk. He had a whole different vibe to him. I didn't know what was coming, but my spider sense told me it was big. I could feel the energy shifting.

"What's your why, Jesse?" Brother Christopher asked in a low, forceful way.

"My why?"

He was waiting for me to respond.

"My why?" I repeated.

"Yes," Brother Christopher said. "What's your why?"

What's My Why?

"The greatest challenge in life is discovering who you are. The second greatest is being happy with what you find."

—UNKNOWN

Back at the Hachette Offices

"So, what'd you tell him?" Kate asks.

I break eye contact with her and look around the room. And then I get up to stretch my legs. We've been in the conference room for an hour.

"I didn't tell him the real reason," I finally say. "That's part of the problem."

I explain that my intentions were pure in the sense I wanted to go up there and get the full-on monk experience, but deep down I know I went there to write a book.

"They knew you might write a book," she says, reading my mind. "That's not a problem."

I assumed the monks knew, but that's not really the issue either. The issue is it doesn't feel authentic—almost like I skipped a step. **There's an old adage, "authenticity over everything,"** and it's ringing in my ear. I pace back and forth a bit to get the circulation going. I'm thinking. And Kate watches me think.

Finally I sit back down.

"I'm just not sure," I say. "I don't know if there's a book here."

She wants me to continue...I want me to continue... But...

"I do have this," I say, sliding my journal across the table.

Kate pulls it closer, opens it, and begins to read my first entry: "If I Were to Die Tomorrow."

March 2017 —

I'm on the plane heading to the monastery and some clown is sitting next to me in 2B. He wants to chat. I don't want to chat. So rather than talk, I'm going to write the first entry of my journal. I think he's trying to read what I'm writing. He's pretending to stretch his neck and turning it back and forth. I can feel his eyes trying to catch a glimpse. I don't care...I promised myself I'd keep a detailed record at New Skete so I can refer back to it years later. Who knows, maybe it'll be something I can hand down to my kids? Maybe there will be some wisdom I can share with others. Maybe it will be a waste of time. But there's only one way to find out and it's been my modus operandi in everything—**start the process and stay in the game. Whether it's a business venture, big race, or a new challenge, I've always had a "get your foot in the door and figure the rest out later" attitude.**

I'm ready for this adventure—I think. I don't really have a plan, I'm just going to try to stick it out, but I know it won't be easy. Nothing worthwhile is. As I sit here on the plane I'm feeling ready. Ready to enter into a monk's life—let's see what they've got.

But for some reason I'm also feeling emotional right now—really emotional. Maybe it's the fear of being away from my wife and children and having no contact. It's not like I have a bad gut feeling about this, it's more like I can't rely on my gut these days. I'm not in tune with it. Technology and life's pace have stripped me of my spiritual intuition. My spider senses I've relied on so heavily my whole life in business and personally have faded.

So instead, crazy thoughts have been flooding into my head for the last twenty-four hours. What am I thinking? I'm thinking the worst-case scenario. I have feelings of guilt for leaving. What if something happens to my kids and I'm not home to prevent it? What if something happens to Sara? What if something happens to me? And if something were to happen to me, wouldn't that be the most selfish thing...A tragedy as the result of me wanting to expand my sandbox is not how I want to go out...

If I Were to Die Tomorrow...

I'd miss the laughter of my children.

I'd miss my wife's hands, amazing eyes, and soft touch.

I'd miss my friends and family so much.

I'd miss everything I wanted to accomplish but ran out of time.

I'd miss the adrenaline rush of life.

If I were to die tomorrow would anyone care in a hundred years? Would have I done enough in life? Would I have regrets? Would I be remembered as the man I want to be? Did I give 100 percent to everything I did? Did I maximize the time I had, or did I waste it? Did I spend my time doing the things that matter the most and with the people who matter the most? Did I try my hardest? Did I keep my word? Did I live with honor? Did I live life to the fullest?

I must live as if I'm going to die tomorrow...

Back at Kate's Office

"This is good," Kate says as she turns the page.

"Thanks, I wrote that on my way. On the plane. Right from my heart."

"Do you mind if I keep reading?"

PART II
The Diary

The door to the monastery. It's going to be an interesting trip.

DAY 1

An Adult Time-Out

"It is in being alone where you find your strength.
Not in others."
—UNKNOWN

In college, on the first day of the semester, professors handed out a syllabus outlining their class for the entire year. We aptly called this syllabus day. I loved it. It literally was a nothing day except for some getting to know you type stuff. And I guess you could call today my monk syllabus day, except I didn't get a sense of what my stay will be like. No one gave me a syllabus. I'm still in the dark.

It's 9:30 p.m. and I'm in my tiny ass room that smells like a closet at my grandma's house. There's an energy here—and I feel it. It feels like some really smart things have been contemplated between these walls. But it's quiet (INSANELY QUIET) and it's dark and spooky. There isn't enough space in my room for me to unpack so I'm going to live out of my suitcase. The room next to mine has a small fridge so I was able to offload all my fruit and veggies.

It feels like I got here days ago.

There's absolutely nothing to do. And literally everything and anything electronically related doesn't work. No phone, no Internet, no texts. Nothing. It's like the Russians used an electromagnetic pulse on the monastery as a mock test of their cyber strength. And it worked.

But there's a part of me that feels free. My phone is attached to me at all times. It's almost become a body part. And so what if shit is going to voicemail right now, emails are being unreturned, and a friend's photo of himself drinking a Corona on Facebook is going un-liked. It's okay. Really—it is.

Brother Christopher, who is my point person or point monk, told me there's one landline for emergencies I can use if needed. What kind of emergencies is he talking about? Avalanche? Survivalists? Wolf attacks? Silent freak-outs from guests?

Maybe I should back up a minute...

I'm at a monastery with eight monks, an intern named Lenny, Josh the Cook who comes a few times a week, and me, that's it. Four of the monks have been here for FIFTY YEARS! FIFTY YEARS. We have very little in common. Scratch that...We have nothing in common. I haven't even been on earth for fifty years. The monastery sits on Two Top Mountain in upstate New York on the Vermont border. It consists of a one-story building where the monks sleep and eat and two churches: the big one I saw on my tour and a smaller chapel. The buildings are made of barn board painted a rusty red. The monks built the monastery themselves.

The plan is to stay here for fifteen days. And time moves as fast as seventh period in grammar school up here. But I should be here long enough to reap the benefits and wisdom of the monks. I feel like the time in isolation will allow me to dig deep inside myself and find whatever it is I'm seeking. I'm giving myself a digital fast. I'm trying to unlock some secrets to make my life better and share them with others. I'm adding another experience to my life résumé.

I didn't have a ton of preconceived notions before I came, but I thought there'd be a lot more people at the monastery, like sixty or something. I'm not sure why I thought that, I just equated "monastery" with large community. I also thought that "monk" meant shaved head. I was wrong on both. And these are Christian monks, not Buddhist—the monks refer to each other as "brothers," and all of the brothers have dogs. And not just any dogs, but big German shepherds that obey their every command in a way I've never seen. Like, the monks can just look at the German shepherds and they respond—total control.

That said, there are eleven adult German shepherds here in total.

Eleven dogs, eight monks, a cook, an intern, and ME.

I'm in my room alone. I have no idea what to do. None.

I'm lying in a bed that's about the size of a cot in a room the monks call a "cell" and for good reason—it feels like a cell. There's a window with a thin white curtain. It's so dark and still outside that it's like before time existed. And here I am...

It's like I'm waiting for a booming voice to say: "AND THEN THERE WAS LIGHT!"

I've been thinking about my kids all day. I need a scream or a yell or a good old-fashioned three-year-old temper tantrum. Something. Anything to stop this silence. *I've never realized how loud silence can be. I miss the chaos. Chaos and noise have become the norm in my life.*

After I arrived Brother Christopher gave me a tour. He's the head monk, the grand poobah of the monastery. He's super nice but doesn't look like a monk. He looks like he should be working the maple syrup tent at the farmer's market: plaid shirt, jeans from Sears and Roebuck, and grimy work boots. But he seems like a hip monk. He's oozing with wisdom. I get the sense he could give some good advice, the kind only a mom can give. I don't know, but as far back as I can remember my mother never misled me. My mom always knew the outcome of things before they happened. And Brother Christopher gives off the same type of vibe.

And one of the first things he asked me was: What's my why...

I keep thinking about it.

Why? Why am I here? Why do we do anything? Why do we spend eighty-plus hours a week working? What's my why?

After our tour he gave me a printout of our daily schedule:

7:15–8:15—Prayer in the morning
8:30—Silent Breakfast
10:00–12:15—Work
12:30—Dinner
1:00—Reflection
2:00–5:00—Work
5:00—Service
6:00—Light Meal
7:00—Reflection / Sleep

The schedule was helpful, but it doesn't shed any light on what I'm going to be doing.

I got excited when Brother Christopher mentioned they have a training center. A monk training center—F yeah...I'm looking forward to getting into all of that. He didn't give me any details, but it sounds cool. I'm here to grow, and I'm treating this time very differently than a vacation; I'm here to work on my inner monk—not my tan. *I've taken enough vacations in my life, and as I get older I find myself wanting experiences instead. I want to do the monks' version of push-ups, pull-ups, and sit-ups. I not only want to learn how to meditate, I want to be doing ultra-meditation by the time I leave.*

I've heard that some monks know how to vary their body temperatures using a myriad of meditation techniques. If they wants, they can test me outside of their training center by making me sit in the snow for hours and teach me how to visualize the heat coming from within my soul. I want to discover how the power of the mind can influence the conscience. I don't want get ahead of myself, but traveling to another dimension might be on my monk wish list. I'm ready to do whatever they want me to do, and I'm willing go to any lengths.

Is that my why? To train with the monks? It's definitely part of it.

An hour after my tour Turney told me he had to go. I didn't want him to leave, so I asked the obvious question: Why, what's up? He politely responded that he had "stuff" to attend to and needed to get back home sooner rather than later. I listened as he explained, but the more he spoke, the more honest his words became. And by the end of it he simply said, "I'm sorry, man, but this place is creeping me out. I need to get out of here. Plus, I can just read a book about this stuff."

We hugged it out, and he was on his way.

Turney had a point; there are a lot of self-help books on happiness, being present, and getting more out of life. However, I don't think you can master anything from reading a book or watching a seminar. All these "Here Are Five Simple Steps" books provide good insight, but unless you take action—nothing happens. Plus, many of the authors of these books have never actually done what they write about. They just write about it. So here I am.

Once Turney peeled out of the parking lot and I got situated, Brother Christopher came back to check on me. We got to chatting, and he said he had another question for me. He looked at me with eyes that were so peaceful it was disturbing. I started to get a pit in my stomach and my enthusiasm for the monk training center vanished. I thought he was about to ask if I wanted to join or make a pledge or give some kind of commitment. Or the VOW of silence...

I didn't know what he was going to say.

"Tell me, are you happy, Jesse?"

I was about to answer when he appeared to drift away in thought. He was standing there almost in a self-hypnotized state; it was like he's mastered meditation on demand. He stood perfectly still for several seconds with his eyes closed. And when he finally opened them a minute later he looked directly at me, like into my soul.

"St. Paul once said there's no difference between contentment and happiness," he said. "Are you happy, Jesse?"

I thought to myself: *Well, Brother Christopher, I am actually very happy, except I'm not that happy right now because it's too quiet and I'm a bit freaked out. There's no one around and I feel like the boredom is going to get to me real quick. Maybe it already has.*

Instead I told him I think I'm happy, but I immediately switched the conversation. I wasn't ready to get too deep, too soon. I have a hard time going deep, especially with a stranger, or for that matter with anyone. Sara says I'm "challenged" when it comes to expressing my emotions. For the first several years of our marriage she'd ask me how I was feeling and I'd always say, "I don't know," which would inevitably lead to an argument. After about three years of this, Sara had an epiphany while driving and pulled off to the side of the road and thought to herself, he really doesn't know how he feels!

She started trying everything to help me get in touch with my emotions. Ultimately, she reverted to using insane sports analogies. She'd say, "Honey, in tennis how would you feel if you hit the ball and someone didn't hit it back?" And then she'd say, "This is how I feel when I'm talking about my feelings and you don't say anything. I'm looking for a good rally."

I think she meant "volley," but I got the point.

But is not knowing sufficient? Should I be exploring to know? Why don't I know how I feel sometimes? I've always shrugged my shoulders when asked. I can only imagine how frustrating that must be for Sara. I've got some work to do.

So anyway, to avoid going deep I changed the topic with Brother Christopher to something I'm very comfortable with—running—and asked if there were any good places to jog. I'm down to do anything the monks ask me to do, but if I can't get an hour or so of running in a day I'll definitely go berserk. I've run virtually every day for the last twenty-five years, 9,125 straight days, over 36,000 miles. So I'm not stopping now.

Plus, *I'm a big believer that you have to carve some time out of each day to do the things you love to do. It's my own rule that I call the "three-hour rule." You take three hours a day for yourself to do what YOU want to do.*

That time is cumulative. It can be going for a walk, watching TV, reading, whatever. But when you're in that time you don't feel guilty that you're not with your family, at work, or doing something else. If you don't take time for yourself— you'll resent the people who are taking those things away from you. I don't want to resent the monks, so I must run.

Brother Christopher told me I could run up and down the private road, which seems like a very long driveway. He said it's about .8 miles to the end, but I shouldn't go beyond that. There are two mobile homes at the end that have dogs that are extremely territorial. "DO NOT GO NEAR THEM."

Didn't need to tell me twice; I'm not much of a dog person even when they're friendly. It's not that I don't like dogs—we just don't click—me and dogs. Brother Christopher said aside from the private road there are also marked trails through the woods, but with the snow and the concern about bears... "I wouldn't recommend that."

Yeah, I'm not really a bear person either...

So basically, I'm trapped on the property.

"Enjoy your time and if you need anything just come find me."

He reminded me we start tomorrow at 7:15 a.m. with service, prayer, and reflection.

I looked at my watch. It was only 7:15 p.m.

"What should I do for the next twelve hours?"

Brother Christopher looked deep into my soul one last time.

"THINK," he said. "Sit and THINK."

I sat on my bed and stared at the wall. I just sat there, partially because he told me to and partially because there was NOTHIING else to do—no Netflix, no Instagram, no kids. But my stay up here is a time to reexamine my life—right? I mean

I invest in reevaluating my businesses all the time, why not dig deep into myself? And yet now it feels like a homework assignment given on a Friday afternoon. Can you reexamine something you're reexamining? Regardless, by 7:30 p.m. I was thinking I might go insane.

I decided to change my mind-set and jump-start my spiritual journey with some meditation. Let's make the best of this. I've never really meditated before, but my friend Brian Koppelman suggested I take a course on transcendental meditation several years ago. The course took two days to complete, and it was one-on-one training. I completed the course but didn't meditate beyond that. I Googled transcendental meditation before I left to get refreshed.

My instructor had explained that because we're so accessible, all the information that comes at us often creates overload. That's where meditation comes into play. Meditation has widely been viewed as one of the best tools to calm your mind and free up mental energy. It slows down the brain and gives it a much-needed rest.

Transcendental meditation, or TM as it's referred to, is the choice of many celebrities, I've heard. Oprah, Jerry Seinfeld, Clint Eastwood...Clint Eastwood? Really? But artists and many successful businesspeople swear by it too. It's a simple and effortless way of settling your mind that focuses around a one-word mantra you're given in training. You focus exclusively on your mantra and block everything else out to slow down the mind. I was told the best practices are two sessions of twenty minutes each a day.

My TM coach gave me my mantra when we met. It's a made-up word so it doesn't stimulate any visual or emotional connection when you focus on it. My mantra is exclusive to me and I'm not allowed to disclose it to anyone—not even my journal. It's supposed to be personal and private. But my mantra sounds like the name of a sushi restaurant.

God, I wish I had some sushi right now.

And today was my first meditation in years.

I shut off the lights and got comfortable in my old monk chair, set the timer on my phone for twenty minutes, and then closed my eyes. Immediately, I got bombarded by thoughts as I tried to focus on my mantra. What are my kids doing right now? How's my wife doing? Will Millsap resign with the Hawks? It was a constant stream of everything and anything attacking my mantra.

But I kept trying.

With my eyes closed I tried to block out the thoughts, but it wasn't working. After what felt like thirty minutes I started wondering why my timer hadn't beeped yet. Maybe I didn't set it properly? I wanted to check but instead kept repeating my mantra over and over for what felt like another ten minutes. I was just waiting for the beeper. After those ten minutes passed, there was still no ding to end the session. At this point I knew something was wrong with the alarm. I debated opening my eyes to check, but it felt like cheating.

And then finally I gave in.

I slowly opened my right eye to peek at the clock resting on my lap: 3:47 and ticking...

Are you kidding me?

What felt like an hour or more was only three minutes and forty-seven seconds? Tom Brady can score three touchdowns in 3:47, Joey Chestnut can eat twenty-five hotdogs in 3:47, and Alan Webb can run a mile in 3:47. And I can't even meditate for

My thinking chair.

that long. Am I that affected by the pace of the real world that I can't calm my mind for just three minutes?

The next thing I did was pull out my calculator to figure out the total time I have left at the monastery. I multiplied fifteen days by twenty-four hours by sixty minutes: 21,600 more minutes of nothingness left to go. I'm never going to make it.

The bell tower.

DAY 2
Learning the Ropes

*"Life is really simple, but we insist on making
it complicated."*
— CONFUCIUS

7:08 a.m.

"Don't be late for the prayer service," Brother Christopher had
said.

It was my only instruction last night. Each service of prayer,
meditation, and reflection lasts about seventy-five minutes and
takes place in the sanctuary. I plan on going to every single one,
two to three times a day. Whatever they got. And I won't be late.
This is why I'm here.

But I woke up feeling like Gilligan on *Gilligan's Island*.
Trapped. Stranded. Helpless. And nothing looks familiar. I feel so
out of place. And I just want to get off the island.

"What are you doing here anyway, Jesse?" Billy said to me.
*"You could be home in bed watching March Madness. Perhaps
we should cut this stupid idea of yours short."*

Oh, now is probably a good time to introduce you to Billy.
Billy is what I call the bully who lives inside my head—all of our
heads. He's our biggest enemy. He always rears himself at big
moments and tries to talk us out of things. It's the self-doubt

that likes to take the easy way out. And Billy the Bully isn't shy about his opinions. He'll tell me every reason why I shouldn't go for that run or why I should put work off until later and start that diet tomorrow. He's the single greatest obstacle to success.

I think we all have a bully inside our head. Sometimes we can quiet him down, and sometimes he becomes all too loud and powerful. And this is the most dangerous thing about the bully in my head—he gets stronger as I get weaker. The last thing he said to me before I started getting ready for this morning was: "*Fine. We'll go to this first service, but we're here on a trial basis.*" He's already rationalizing and planting the excuse seed in my head. He's giving me an out. That's what our mental bullies do. They feed doubt and insecurity between our ears.

I took a peek outside to try to quiet my mind when: BONG! BING! DONG!

Oh shit, I said to myself. The bells.

I had to get to service.

And just as I started to tie my shoes: BONG! BING! DONG!

No way was I going to be late to my first service. After a quick wash-up I hustled out the door. The bells rang again. The bell tower is four feet from my room. All that's missing is a guy with a hump. And the tower is not for show. It's the world's biggest alarm clock. Brother Christopher warned me the bells would ring five minutes before every service indicating we should head to the church. He also gave me a friendly heads-up that the bells might be loud.

Might be loud?

THEY'RE SHAKING THE EARTH THEY'RE SO LOUD.

As I jogged over to the church I thought my eardrums were going to explode: BONG! BING! DONG! The sound could wake up the dead, which by the way there are a number of at the monastery. Right outside of my room's window is the monk cemetery—a dozen or so little wooden crosses sticking out of the snow. That's the view from my bed—comforting.

As I ran toward the church door, I looked up in the tower and saw Brother Luke. He's in charge of the bells. He's strong and husky looking. He's wearing huge headphones like the ones the guys use to land 747s to block the noise. I live five feet away from the tower and the monks gave me nothing? I covered my ears with the palms of my hands and dug my left ear into my shoulder for more protection as I flew by the bell tower toward the sanctuary.

I swung open the door to the church. I made it just in time—SUCCESS.

The church is called "Holy Wisdom Church," and it's beautiful. Polished marble tile floor, wooden chairs ornately carved, candles and latticework, and a lot of paintings. High on the walls are life-sized portraits of famous religious figures, like a heavenly Hall of Fame. They even have names under the paintings, so you know who you're looking at. I didn't know who most of them were, a lot of Russian guys and popes from the Middle Ages or something like that. But a few I did know, like Mother Theresa, King David, and Moses.

The church was pretty dark this morning with no lights on. The only sunlight enters through the stained-glass windows. The sanctuary is also filled with smoke as the monks burn incense at the services. Think majestic with a mysterious vibe—that's the church. It seats about sixty people at capacity. But today, there were only two other non-monks in attendance. I guess the services are open to the public. I tried to give the other two civilians a "let's do this" nod to fire them up, but they weren't interested. It was just like athletes stretching and going through a pre-game ritual; these two already had their own pre-service vibe going on. Or they were just ignoring me because they immediately put their heads down—deep thought.

At 7:15 the door at the rear of the church opened and the monks entered the sanctuary one by one in silence. They were draped in long black robes from head to toe, and two of them wore big crosses around their necks. They immediately took their seats.

Two of the older monks sat in the rear corner while the others formed a choir and sat in a small semicircle in the middle of the church. They had music stands like you'd find in an elementary school auditorium for their prayers and song charts. All of the monks participated in the chanting and prayers. And in addition to the monks there were three nuns in the choir as well. I sat in a pew across from them. Alone.

I kept hearing them say Jesus, but I didn't follow anything else. My mind wandered. I tried to stay focused, but I thought about random shit. I mean, really random. And my thoughts were like an out-of-order slide show—do any of these monks have tattoos—how long will it take to grow my hair back—are monks even allowed to have tattoos—what if my hair grows in straight— can any of these monks make a foul shot—which of the three nuns is the fastest sprinter? Yeah, that kind of random.

The service was filled with song, psalms, and prayers, all chanted in a very melodic and ancient tone—it felt very religious but a bit haunting. It was great to be a congregant, but I felt more like a spectator than a participant. However, once I got used to it—the sound was like a massage for the soul. I closed my eyes for a second to be at one with the harmony and the soothing sounds. I felt good—real good—so good. I could listen to that all day. And then...

The service was over. The monks were filing out of the church.

What happened?

I fell asleep.

My spiritual journey didn't get off to a great start.

After service, Brother Christopher officially introduced me to Lenny the Intern. They stopped by my room together. Lenny is twenty-three years old and interning at the monastery for about six months. Today is the start of his second week. There's no polite way of saying this: Lenny reminds me of the serial killer in *Fargo*—big dirty work boots, flannel shirt tucked into Levi 501 blue jeans. And...a stone-cold look in his eyes.

Brother Christopher told me Lenny the Intern was sleeping in the cell next to mine. Great. When I heard that I instinctively checked my doorknob to see if it had a lock. It does. I was told Lenny is a professional intern—whatever that means. It sounds like he goes from community to community interning. He just got off a six-month stint at an Indian reservation. I'm not so sure Lenny has showered in between intern gigs as he looked like he just came out of a dusty western movie.

Once the introduction was complete, I tried to chat it up.

After all, we'd be monk-mates for the next two weeks.

"Hey Lenny, how are you doing?"

He just stared at me.

"You like it up here?"

Lenny faced me but directed his eyes to the top of my head. He was staring two inches above my eyes. What the fuck, the guy was intentionally not making eye contact. I was just trying to be friendly. And this guy was staring at me like a prizefighter trying to intimidate his opponent right before they touch gloves and start the fight.

"I'm excited for my stay. Let me know if you need anything while I'm here."

Lenny the Intern just glared and then walked out. When he got halfway to the doorway he turned and stared at the top of my head again and then left. No words, like nothing.

Lenny—Lenny—Lenny...

There's a Native American proverb that makes me think of Lenny. It goes like this: An older Cherokee is teaching his grandson about life, but the boy explains there's a fight going on inside of him between two wolves. One is evil—he is anger, envy, sorrow, regret, greed, arrogance, self-pity, guilt, resentment, inferiority, lies, false, pride, superiority, and ego. But the other wolf is good—he is joy, peace, love, hope, serenity, humility, kindness, benevolence, empathy, generosity, truth, compassion, and faith.

It's explained to the boy that the fight is going on not just inside of him but in every other person as well.

So the grandson asked, "Which wolf will win?"

The old Cherokee said, "The one you feed."

I think I know which wolf Lenny is feeding.

Maybe Lenny feels threatened by me? Maybe he thinks I'm an intern too? Maybe he thinks I'm getting too much attention?

Maybe he's just an asshole? Whatever the case is, I made a mental note: Stay the fuck away from Lenny the Intern.

I organized my room and spent most of the day touring the monastery on my own and trying to learn the ins and outs of the place. No one has instructed me to do anything yet. I haven't even been here for twenty-four hours and am already thinking about when it'll be over. I miss my family.

At lunch I realized that monks do meals quite differently than I'm used to. It's like their meals are dyslexic. First off, they call lunch "dinner." And they call the evening meal "supper." So, they have one big meal around noon (dinner) and then a light meal at night (supper). When I asked what they call breakfast, they said, "What do you mean? We call it breakfast."

Okay then.

Today's menu for supper was soup and salad. That's it. I ladled soup into a bowl and put some salad on a plate. All of the monks and Lenny were already seated around the long rectangular dinner table. I found an empty chair and sat next to Brother Christopher. Normally I'm fairly comfortable in new situations, but this was different.

At the table, each of the monks introduced themselves. There are eight who live at the monastery, and I'm guessing the average age is sixty. But it's a young and vibrant sixty. There's a ninth monk who lives at an assisted living facility. I think they said his name is Peter. And the word is—avoid getting sucked into a conversation with him because he doesn't have an off button.

I sat with my soup/salad combo and checked if anyone else was eating yet.

They weren't. And that's when the introductions started. By the time the monks were done saying a quick hello I'd forgotten all of their names. But what I can say about them is they almost all have gray hair and beards. And they all smile like they know something I don't.

Next, they wanted to know a little bit more about me. I led with the family bio and told them how grateful I was to be allowed to stay with them. I'm assuming Kate pulled a string to get me up here, so I wanted them to know it was an honor. I told them I was involved with the Atlanta Hawks and all I got were blank stares. I threw out a couple of players' names, but I think that confused them even more. Right after I explained what I meant, one of the monks, I think his name is Stavros, said he once went to an Expos game. Not really the same thing, I told him. The Expos are baseball. And they don't exist anymore. The Hawks play basketball. And they play on national TV. He didn't seem to care, but it was cool because it led to a deeper conversation.

Stavros grew up in Washington, D.C. He was from a typical middle-class family and decided to become a monk in college after studying Eastern religion. His mother was so against him becoming a monk, she said she was going to fly up to stop him. When Brother Stavros heard, he had her paged at the airport and told her not to come. He knew in his heart what he wanted to do. I guess he was right. He's been a monk since Lyndon Johnson was president.

I can relate to that—there have been times in my life when I've just known something. When I was twenty-two years old I wrote and sang the theme song for the New York Knicks called "Go NY Go." It was a song the Knicks played to fire up the crowd at Madison Square Garden after the team went on a rally. The Knicks shot a video with big New York celebs to support the song. And it caught fire. The song reached number one on New York radio. As the song rose to fame, so did I. I made appearances on local TV stations, signed copies of the song in stores, and was escorted to the front of the line at the hottest nightclubs. I was on top of the world. Yet, despite the meteoric rise of the song and all of the attention, I was dead-ass broke.

In fact, I didn't even have a place to live. At the time I was living on the floor of my friend's apartment and my time was about up—like yesterday. As luck would have it, he told me as of Monday, which was in three days, I had to be out. Rather than panic, that weekend I opted to go to a bachelor party on the Jersey Shore. Not having a place to live could wait until Monday. After my friends and I checked into the one hotel room we were all sharing, we immediately hit the local dive bar for happy hour. After about an hour of light food and beer with my friends, I started chatting with this gal at the bar as I waited for my gin and tonic. She was a very attractive brunette with a sinister smile. She had a quiet confidence that made you like and respect her. Her name was Melissa Katz.

It was just regular bar conversation—bullshitting. But five minutes into my wrap she asked me where I lived. I explained my situation and told her I just moved back from Cali. And as of Monday I had nowhere to go.

"Really," she said.

She asked the bartender for a pen and wrote her address on the back of a napkin.

"You can stay with me and my roommate Alyssa if you get stuck," she said.

"Is that a real offer?"

"That's an emergency offer."

As the night progressed, the traveling bachelor party was ready for the next leg. I wasn't sure I'd ever see her again. But when Monday rolled around I started thinking through my living options and realized things were pretty dire. This could easily be classified as an "emergency." So, at 8:00 a.m. as my Jersey Girl was heading out to work, I showed up at her apartment with my one bag of all my possessions.

I lived in her living room on the couch for six months. If she had a playdate, I'd stay out of the apartment until the guy left. I'd usually wait in the lobby. It was a sitcom in the making, and we became good friends.

As it turned out, her dad was a high-profile business mogul in New York and Philly who was also involved in the sports business. He was highly respected and someone I looked up to. We became instant pals, and he served as an early mentor for my business career. So when I was faced with my first real business decision at twenty-two years old, I went to him.

I had an interesting dilemma. With the success of the Knicks song, I knew I was potentially onto something big. Other NBA teams were calling me to write theme songs and advertising slogans for them. I saw a clear path to success. However, I had no money to pay the studio, singers, lawyers, and everyone else I needed to make this happen. Shit, I didn't even have rent money. And without the ability to do demos, I'd be out of business.

I was desperate. In an effort to raise money I went to a big New York music manager who offered me $10,000 for 10 percent of my future earnings—all of them. He basically wanted to buy a piece of ME (like a stock) for life...and at twenty-two years old with no money, I was seriously considering his offer. Ten thousand dollars was all the money in the world.

I called my roommate's dad.

After some back-and-forth calls, we scheduled a meeting at his penthouse apartment in Sutton Place. When I arrived I was greeted by a staff worker who told me Mr. Katz was expecting me.

"Feel free to make your way in," he said.

Since I didn't really know what "make your way in" meant, I started to wander around the apartment, you know...checking the place out. Whoa, this place was amazing. Colorful carpets with amazing designs, antique sculptures and art that looked like it had big insurance policies. I felt like a tourist at the Louvre. As I was staring at art that looked like it should have a security guard by it, I heard a noise coming from what appeared to be the master bedroom, so I headed that way.

"Jesse, come on in, son."

I followed the voice through the bedroom and into a workout area where I could see Lewis getting out of the swimming pool. He was butt-ass naked. Totally—NUDE. I'm not sure what was more surprising—that he had no shame or that he had a giant indoor swimming pool in his apartment.

"Sit down, son. I'm a bit rushed this morning, so why don't you tell me what's on your mind?"

"Well, I have...," I said, keeping my eyes laser focused on his eyes. "I, um, have a-ah."

Finally he threw on some skimpy shorts and grabbed his sneakers.

"Oh, don't mind me," he said. "I'm just getting a quick quarter mile in while I'm still fresh from the water," as he headed over to the treadmill.

I'd heard about eclectic wealthy folk, but I'd never met one. And Lewis was more than eclectic; he was brilliant, a badass and genius. Who gives a fuck if he likes to swim nude and work out in skimpy shorts? He'd earned that right. As I started to talk again he stepped on the treadmill and hit the start button. All of a sudden he had a very serious tone as he ran.

"You know what, Jesse, I'd give it all back...the pool, the art, the apartment, EVERYTHING to have the one thing you have."

"Me? I have $128. I'm broke. What's that?"

He looked me dead in the eye as he ran.

"Youth."

"Youth?"

"Yes. The process, the thrill of the unknown, the long playing field ahead...it all comes with youth. As you get older the game gets shorter. You, my friend, have hundreds of experiences in front of you. Your future is a huge canvas to paint on, and I'd trade it all to have that paintbrush back in my hand. Enjoy every minute of the process."

"Wow," was all I could say.

"What you're going through is the process. This decision, these moments, the unknown. You're an entrepreneur, son, and big decisions like this are part of the process."

Almost thirty years later that conversation was clear in my mind as I was talking with Brother Stavros. And as I get older, it holds more true. ***Very often the process is more valuable than the outcome. As you struggle in business, with goals, at work—it's hard to appreciate the journey. However, it is the journey that makes us feel the most alive.*** That's why I'm here. I love Turney, but he left. He chose to read it instead of live it.

I'm lucky that Lewis's message resonated with me at an early age.

We only have two kinds of memories in our life, ones that we can't control and the ones that we create. The ones that we can't control are things that just happen during our lives that leave an indelible memory—like 9/11, the O.J. Simpson car chase, our son falling and losing a tooth, etc. We remember those moments with complete clarity, but we had nothing to do with them. The other kind of moments are the ones that we control and create ourselves—running our first marathon, our first date, etc. When you're young, you have so many opportunities to create positive memories. And that's what Lewis was getting at. **The memories we create of our own accord are the paint-brushes...life is the canvas.**

Lewis continued his workout while we continued our conversation. And yes—he was running extremely fast in his skimpy shorts. And I needed help with my business. I was about to sell 10 percent of Jesse Itzler to this music manager. Lewis adjusted his treadmill to a 12 on the incline meter and was slowly climbing up a mock mountain.

"I want you to go past the excitement, Jesse, past the passion, past the ego, and dig into your GUT."

"Okay."

"Now tell me...Do you believe in your heart of hearts in this sports music thing you're doing?"

"I think so.

"NO, THAT'S NOT ENOUGH! Jesse, I want to know, would you bet the entire farm on this concept? I don't want to know 'can' you make this work but 'WILL' you make this work. That means no matter what is thrown at you."

His words sounded like a wise football coach pumping up the team at halftime. I thought about it for a few moments and then responded.

"Yes sir, without question I WILL make this work."

"Then fuck the $10k, son."

Lewis got off the treadmill, grabbed a towel, and patted me on the shoulder.

"It's up to you to make it happen now," he said, leaving for his meeting. Well, he got dressed first, but then he left for his meeting.

As I sat across from Brother Stavros, I wondered if we had the same exact feeling. He knew he was a monk. I knew I had a great idea combining music with professional sports. We were probably about the same age when we made those decisions. And thankfully, we trusted our guts.

When I asked Brother Stavros if he's happy, he smiled and said, "Even better, I'm content."

I told him I was excited to get started with my monk training.

He just smiled. Monks sure do smile a lot.

After supper was over, all of the monks stood to face a wall that has a painting of Jesus. As soon as they got up, I got up. Since I don't know the daily routine, I'm trying to mimic everything the monks do. I want to blend in and be respectful of their traditions. It's like a giant game of Simon Says and all the monks are Simon. I've used this technique in business, and it has worked. When you're young you have to laugh when everyone at the table laughs to get the deal done. Even if the joke isn't funny. When you don't have to laugh at those jokes any more, you've made it.

So, they started to pray.

I started to pray.

Or maybe I should say I started acting like I was praying.

No one ever taught me how to pray.

And I got nothing against JC, it's just that I could count on one finger the number of times I was in a church. I don't know much about the Christian faith. I mean, I know the basics, the story of Christmas, being hung on the cross, and rising from the dead, but my brain isn't wired toward religion. If you started talking to me about an in-depth history or the different orders or denominations you might as well be speaking to me about quantum mechanics—I know nothing. Even the meaning(s) of prayer is lost on me. And there we were—praying. But I have to say, there was something really nice about standing with a table full of men and listening to them say the words with conviction. Amen...

By 8 p.m. I was solo again in my cell.

I'm not getting discouraged because tomorrow's the big day! I was told I'm going to shadow Brother Thomas at the training facility. That's like a tap on the shoulder. And I'm ready! I want the hardcore meditation and spiritual shit to kick in. I'm excited to take a look inside the monks' toolbox. I want to understand how they've mastered dedication, discipline, and single-minded devotion for thousands of years. **Monks have carried down traditions and philosophies that require sheer determination. That's a skill set you can stuff into your pocket and bring with you into any endeavor.** And monks make the courageous decision to leave behind the world as we know it and devote their entire lives to a higher cause. To me—that's impressive.

Who can't afford to add a little bit more honor and courage into their lives?

Also, though it may sound ironic, I believe monks have completely captured the idea of freedom—free from everything—distractions and attachments. It's like they've unlocked the secret of life's meaning. Who knows? Maybe by the time I'm done here, they'll have given me the keys. But just to be clear, I'm not on some existential search. I don't have to do anything other than look at my kids to know the meaning of life. And I'm not looking to serve God (I don't want to tell Brother Christopher or any of the other monks this, not yet), but I am mesmerized by the monks' calmness and appreciation of their simple lives.

I can't wait to kick this thing off tomorrow.

DAY 3
The Distractor

"He who conquers others is strong; he who conquers himself is mighty."
—LAO TZU, *DAO DE JING*

"Beat the bells," I said to myself when I woke up. I wanted to get to the church before the first ring. It was still early, so I went outside. I saw the sun rise. I mentally prepared for the day as I took a four-mile walk. It's not always easy to prepare for the unknown, which the training center was, but I tried to enjoy the pristine setting.

That wasn't easy because I had the dogs on my mind. It's hard to explain what it feels like being airdropped into a completely new setting with so many dogs—I think there are eleven full-grown, trained German shepherds. And they may or may not like me. I'm not convinced all of the dogs know my scent yet, and I kept thinking one of them would think I was an intruder on the property if they saw me walking. While the monks have full mastery of their dogs, and the dogs rarely venture more than fifty yards from their masters, none of them are on a leash. So until I'm positive all the dogs have fully vetted me, I'm staying on high alert. Let's just say I walked at a very brisk pace today.

Since I just got back to my room, I figured I'd jot something down before I beat the bells.

For starters, it's super cold in my room. There's a gap between the window glass and the window frame that allows the freezing cold mountain air to come right in, which would be great if it were like 84 degrees outside, but it's more like minus four. You could freeze vegetables in here. The angle creates some kind of wind tunnel that's directing the cold to hit me right in the face during my sleep. It's freezing. I had to sleep in my winter jacket last night to stay warm. Despite the cold air, I slept great.

BONG! BING! DONG!

I wore the same thing to church I wore yesterday. Monks are big on function not fashion. In fact, I think they all wore the same clothing that they did yesterday. Nobody seems to care about how they look around here. And I'm still playing Simon Says.

During service I tried to focus on the message, but the training center was interrupting my thoughts. I wondered what kinds of things they do in there. But every time I caught myself prancing around in I-Wonder-What-It's-Like-in-the-Training-Center-Land, I told myself to concentrate on the service. It was a losing battle.

I can't remember a single thing they said in church.

After service I went to the dining room. All of the monks and Lenny the Intern were present and accounted for when I walked in. I said hello to Brother Gregory.

"SHHHHHH," I heard from the whole room in unison.

It was a SILENT MEAL! But nobody told me! There's no sign hanging on the wall that says: SILENT MEAL with a picture of a monk silhouette using a silent finger to the mouth. Some kind of heads-up would have been nice.

When I sat down to eat I held the bottom of my seat and hopped forward to bring my chair closer to the table. The legs of the chair accidentally scrapped across the kitchen floor as it moved one inch and then came to an abrupt halt. It was loud—real loud. The monks, Lenny the Intern, and the dogs all looked up at me. I don't think they were mad, but it felt like when someone turns their head at the movie theater, which is the international sign for SHUT THE FUCK UP.

I didn't mean to make that much noise.

Once I got situated I looked around the room. It was like watching a television show on mute. The monks were slowly bringing their spoons to their mouths and eating their oatmeal. They have perfected the art of eating without the sound of chewing. They did it with such precision and skill that they didn't make a single sound. Not a slurp to be heard. Some stared straight ahead as they ate; others looked down into their bowls. It was pretty freaky. I closed my eyes and imagined the breakfast table at my house. Holy crap. Like an alternate universe!

I wondered what the monks were thinking about, but I couldn't even guess what was going on in their minds. Sometimes I can look at my kids, Sara, a friend, or whomever and without them saying a word I have a pretty good idea what's going on in their head—or at least I think I do. But with the monks, it's like another world. Even eating breakfast they're impressive.

I was starving. And since it was before noon my only choice was apples. I wish my bananas had survived the flight. When my teeth penetrated the skin of the Granny Smith apple it sounded like a huge explosion. Like a fireworks display when they play the *1812 Overture*.

Juice squirted out and landed on the cheek of Brother Thomas. And guess what? He didn't flinch. Total focus. LeBron on the foul line. Swish! As he brought his spoon of oatmeal to his mouth the juice splattered right into his goatee. He just continued to think.

But every other monk looked at me. "SHHHH!" they all said in unison.

Forty seconds later I finally took another bite, but this time I kept the apple in my mouth without chewing. I sat there and pretended I was eating and thinking. I thought if the apple piece stayed in my mouth long enough I could possibly dissolve it, but that might have taken about three weeks. I didn't have that much time, so I decided to hard swallow the enormous piece whole. Bad idea. The apple was stuck in my throat. I mean stuck—Heimlich situation waiting to happen.

I started to breathe through my nose as I continued to hard swallow. I closed my eyes hoping the monks would think I was meditating, not choking on an apple. This lasted for about a minute, and then I started uncontrollably coughing. The good news was the apple dislodged from my throat and I swallowed it; the bad news was the monks realized I wasn't meditating.

Choking can really spoil a silent meal.

I waited another five minutes and decided to give it another shot. I held the apple in my hand and lowered my head again like I was deep in thought. What I was really thinking about was…How in the world am I going to eat this damn apple? After it felt acceptable, like enough time to have a deep reflection passed, I got up. I was super careful to not scrape the chair on the floor.

I ate the apple in my room.

And then finally...finally it was time to head to the training center and shadow Brother Thomas. I had a bounce in my step the whole way there. This is what I'd been waiting for:

THE TRAINING CENTER

DOING THE MONK THING

GETTING DOWN WITH MY INNER SELF.

10:00 a.m.

Brother Thomas was waiting for me at the training center, the Quonset hut–like building. He's young, vibrant, and full of life. He looks like a mixed martial arts fighter. He's on the shorter side but very fit with a goatee and one eye that floats a little bit, so you're never really sure if he's looking at you. My guess is he could choke the life out of me if he wanted, but he talked in a soft, soothing way.

"Are you ready to train?"

"Yes sir."

"Good because we have some feisty ones in there."

Feisty? Not really sure what he was talking about, but I was game for anything.

"Do you like dogs, Jesse?"

"Dogs?"

"Yes, dogs."

"You mean as in dogs?"

"Yes, as in dogs."

The training center isn't for spiritual fitness, it's for training dogs!

The monks train dogs?

Dogs! As in Woof...Woof.

I signed up to be with MONKS—not DOGS. I should have done more research. I can hear Sara now: "Jesse, that's why you read the fine print, honey."

But I'm not a fine print kind of guy.

I followed him inside. The training center is as big as a gymnasium. It's also brand new and state-of-the-art right down to the cushy rubber floor matting and the two-way mirror from the viewing room. There were several dogs in kennels at one end, and they yelped as we walked closer. The place smelled like one gigantic pet store.

But if I had to guess—this place was probably the Madison Square Garden equivalent of dog training centers. There should be banners hanging in the rafters. For a moment I marveled at the structure, wondering what in the hell I was doing there. I don't know whether I was more surprised or disappointed. My monk training will have to wait, I guess.

Brother Thomas opened one of the cages and put a leash on Rainbow, a big, light-colored golden Labradoodle puppy. I don't know—I'm not a dog person, but if I had one I always thought I'd name him or her either Tofu or Broccoli.

Rainbow?

And then Brother Thomas told me I was going to be the "distractor" today. He was going to walk Rainbow around the training center, and I was going to walk ahead of them, cross in front, and do whatever I could to distract her.

"Try and make her lose focus from her goal," he said.

Fifteen minutes before, I had thought I was about to enter into some type of spiritual hell week, a monk's version of the training I did with SEAL. Instead, I was in an airplane hangar–sized kennel being a dog distractor. Regardless, I was going to try to be the best dog distractor that New Skete has ever seen.

It turns out the monks of New Skete are world-famous dog trainers and breeders of German shepherd dogs! And they have a two-year wait list for puppies. Their dog training program has been featured in books, television shows, and numerous articles. Who knew? I guess I would have if I'd done any research before I left. One quick Google search would have resulted in hundreds of links.

Back in the 1970s, when the monks were building the monastery, they adopted a German shepherd, Kyr. The dog was a big hit with monks who were working hard all day putting up the buildings. Instantly, the community fell in love with him. And he fell in love with them.

"He brought joy into their lives," Brother Thomas told me.

When Kyr died unexpectedly a couple of years later, the community was shattered. After some time, one of the monks suggested they set out to find a replacement for their beloved pet. As luck would have it—and there seems to be a lot of luck in the monks' story—that is, if you don't believe in divine intervention—a dog breeder lived not too far away. When they went to see her, she said she'd be happy to give them a dog. In fact, she'd give them two—both breeding-caliber German shepherds. This way they could raise a litter or two and sell the puppies, she said. Always looking for ways to keep the lights burning, the monks went about giving the dog breeding game a try. Back at the monastery, the dogs did what dogs do and, apparently, did it well. Out came one litter after another.

Apparently, the particular type of German shepherd the lady breeder gave them is pretty special—pure German lines—and could sell for a pretty hefty price. It was the beginning of something they couldn't have imagined. Visitors started to remark about how well behaved their German shepherds were. And one of them asked if they'd consider training their dog. The next thing you know they had a training center and a steady stream of customers. It was like any great entrepreneurial journey; they saw a need and filled it.

Above the door of the training center there's a sign that reads: Maurice Sendak Center. Sendak, the author and illustrator of *Where the Wild Things Are*, had a summer cabin nearby and became a good friend of the monks after he purchased one of their German shepherds. His foundation helped with the building of the training center by offering the monastery a matching grant gift. Now, if that's where the story of the monks and their dogs ended it'd have been pretty amazing, but it didn't.

One of their early customers suggested they write a dog-training book. People tell other people they "ought to write a book" all the time, usually at dinner parties, in bars, or in airline seats. So the phrase really doesn't mean a whole lot except if the person who says it happens to be an editor for a publishing company, which their customer was. The monks first book (they have a bunch of them), first published in 1978, is called *How to Be Your Dog's Best Friend*. Some consider it the bible of dog-training books, but the monks would shake their heads at that turn of phrase. Altogether, the monks' dog books have sold in the millions of copies and, in the dog universe, the monks of New Skete are beloved.

I felt honored to be in the presence of these masters. When you're around people who are among the best in the world at what they do, it's enlightening. Their command of the dogs was evident right away. If any of the monks spoke, the dogs responded. They could take a wild party animal like Spuds MacKenzie and in a week or two turn him into a well-behaved private school dog. Training is like a two-and-a-half-week etiquette school for dogs. They come in as barkers/jumpers/bullies and leave like debutants.

Rainbow was at the end of her stay and was walking at Brother Thomas's side like the dogs at the famous Westminster Kennel Club Dog Show. I could have been waving a pork chop around and she wouldn't give me a second look. I walked in front of them and Rainbow checked me out but concentrated on her task at hand. I darted behind them and she didn't even turn her head. I busted out a few jumping jacks—nothing. And then I pulled out my secret weapon—the underarm fart. I put my hand in my armpit and started pumping my elbow against my body making loud farting sounds. This makes every kid laugh and even cracked Brother Thomas a bit, but not Rainbow. The dog was trained.

"Would you like to walk Rainbow?" he asked.

"Nope," I said. "I'm all good."

Later, Brother Thomas and I sat in a private two-way mirror room talking about dogs.

"The biggest mistake people make in training dogs is they concentrate only on the dog. All they're interested in is the end result—that Fido, or Rainbow here, will sit, stay, and roll over when they command them to. Although they might be successful in obtaining those goals, such a technique does not improve the relationship with the dog. And the dog will end up being either unhappy or resentful."

"Dogs can be resentful?"

"Of course."

"So the owner needs to be trained too?"

"Exactly. As it is in life."

"Well, what if we don't have a dog?" I asked half kidding.

"We all must be trained, Jesse. **The power and temptations of the outside world are great. Train yourself from the distractions.** They are the enemies of your goals. Learn to move past the distractions, and you will succeed."

"Like Rainbow?"

"Exactly like Rainbow."

Whoa. I had to chew on that for a second.

It's Day 3, and I'm starting to get some real nuggets of wisdom through the most unlikely scenarios. I never thought about dog training where the owner needs to be trained too. But I didn't come up here to distract dogs. I thought I'd be going through some rigorous mental training. And maybe I am. Maybe I'm in the midst of the ultimate training and don't even know it. Like the Karate Kid. He didn't know it at the time, but waxing Mr. Miyagi's car taught him to become a superior fighter. Maybe by distracting dogs I'm learning the ultimate art of not being distracted. Or maybe I'm overthinking it.

By 2:00 p.m., I was in my room reading Viktor Frankel's *Man's Search for Meaning*. And then at some point I noticed Brother Christopher standing in my doorway. I'm not sure how long he was watching me. Monks seem to just appear, like by astral projection or Star Trek transporter. He stopped by to check on me. As strange as this sounds—it felt nice to see a familiar face. I wanted to chat a little bit. I wasn't ready for him to leave, so I told him I was looking forward to my journey. I thought that was a nice way of saying: Come on, man. Let's crack that monk whip. Give me something more to do...

His response was: *"Every day is a lesson. The key is to listen."*

Huh? At first I didn't understand and I've already noticed the monks talk in spiritual code, but then it dawned on me that I am in fact a terrible listener. I made a note that this is one thing I really have to work on when I get home—LISTENING. But maybe listening has a bigger meaning then simply being quiet and hearing others talk. Perhaps it means being less caught up with yourself and opening up to new opportunities, ideas, and perspectives.

Brother Christopher referenced a wise monk: "When you talk, you are only repeating what you already know. But if you listen, you may learn something new."

At night, as I lay in bed, Billy the Bully wanted to have a little pillow talk. He was quick to remind me that this isn't what I was expecting. I didn't sign up for dogs, so there's no shame in going home early. And besides, my bed at home is much more comfortable than this.

The view from my cell window.

DAY 4
Murder, He Wrote

"Ultimately, we must leave room for mystery."
—THE MONKS OF NEW SKETE

In case something happens to me and you're a detective reading this diary, Lenny the Intern did it. Though my guess is that Lenny is smart enough to destroy any evidence, so maybe this entry is a wasted effort. But...Lenny—way—freaks the monk out of me.

Just the thought of the guy got me thinking about background checks. Do the monks just take in whoever shows up, or do you have to be vetted? I'm thinking background checks may be a really un-monkish thing to do because they're supposed to be loving and accepting of everyone. I started considering the best ways to secretly vet Lenny via the monks. I could ask them—where did Lenny come from—did anyone know Lenny before he got here—can you tell me about Lenny's parents? I mean Lenny could be number one on the FBI's most wanted list and the monks would have no idea. How would they? It's not like they'd see it on TV or hear about it—we're too remote. It's really getting inside of my head.

Case in point...

Late last night I headed to the dining room to see if anyone was around. I couldn't sleep. And when I walked in I saw Lenny.

He was just sitting in a chair staring at the wall. It was like he was meditating but with his eyes open. The guy was zoned out. I saw a book on the table, so I sat down, picked it up, and pretended to read. It was weird to sit so close to someone and not acknowledge each other. Sitting in the same room was like getting on an elevator with Lenny. It's like he's perfectly comfortable treating me like a stranger.

My relationship with Lenny has gotten progressively worse, which is hard to do for two people who don't even talk to each other. But every time he passes me in the hallway, he narrowly misses slamming his shoulder into mine, I think on purpose. His head is down, he looks straight at the floor, and leans into it like he's about to make a shoulder tackle, but each time he misses me by half an inch. It's like he's sending me a message.

Let me put it this way—when Lenny the Intern is around— Billy the Bully goes into hiding.

I kept fake reading as I sat there ten feet from him. I wanted to have a conversation or at least get a reaction. I got up to get some water. I made deliberate noise with the cooler to see if he'd look up. Maybe we could have our first conversation, I thought. But he wasn't fazed by my distraction. He probably already trained with the dogs. So next I cleared my throat, but still I got nothing.

I wanted to call his name, but I knew that wouldn't work. He tunes me out—all the time. When I say simple things like "Lenny, please pass the salt," he ices me. Nothing—no response. Sometimes he just looks at the top of my head and leaves the room. And it's not just me. Lenny isn't responding to the monks either. But when he does speak, which is rare, he yells like a drill sergeant on volume 8. Yesterday Brother Gregory asked him to help with the dishes. And he walked right up to him and screamed, "I'M HAPPY TO DO THE DISHES, BROTHER GREGORY," like he was at a soccer match in Liverpool. Whatever happened to inside voices?

WTF is wrong with this guy?

I stood there looking at him just waiting for a glance or something. He must have known I was trying to catch his eye, but again—nothing. He was wearing the same clothes he always does—every day. And he wears coffee stains, mud splatter, and dog drool like badges of honor. His main job here is to light incense at the services. At the midway point, Lenny comes out of a back room in his Fargo outfit and military-marches to the candles around the church and lights them. Then at the end of the service, he reappears and blows them out. Then he disappears again.

Although Lenny the Intern seems insane, I must say, there's no task too small for the guy. Anything he's asked to do he does without uttering a single word of frustration or giving a hint of objection. Lenny mops the floor, scrubs the church, and cleans the dishes. Hey Lenny, there's dog shit on the lawn. ROGER THAT, Lenny picks it up with his hands. He's a ridiculous worker—the perfect intern. That said, I'm four days in and have yet to hear him really say anything. I'm scared shitless of Lenny the Intern. But the monks love him.

Today was a struggle. I'm dying to get into some deep reflection and mental mastery. It just didn't happen again—nothing really happened. The services were good, but nobody has told me what to do at them, they just threw me in the fire. In a way though it's good as it's forced me to pay close attention and figure it out on my own. They say that's the best way to learn. *My wife always*

tells her employees, "If nobody told you how to do your job, how would you do it?" The results she gets from that are amazing. **Sometimes you have to rip up the playbook, break the mold, and do it your own way.**

After the chanting and reflections around Jesus, today's theme for service was forgiveness. It's something I struggle with. It's not that I live with a lot of resentments, but I have a hard time of letting go when I feel like I've been wronged or betrayed. So it really hit home when Brother Christopher explained that forgiveness was the answer to wasted energy. I really got it. But I'm still pissed at a few people.

This morning after the early service and before I started chores, Billy the Bully thought it was a good idea to check my phone, just in case it started working somehow. He wanted to check email, social media, and see if I could fire off a text. It was like a ten-minute one-sided conversation. He talked and I listened.

I needed to get out of my cell. But since there's no way I was going to run in the woods with the warning of bears and the two territorial dogs at the bottom of the hill, who sound like *Cujo* on a bad day, I decided to walk up and down the private road. It was the only safe option.

The reason I chose to walk instead of run was because I don't want to do laundry here. For starters, I'm not good at laundry (my whites turn pink), but I also don't want to get in anyone's way up here. Last thing I want to do is hog the laundry machine. For that reason, I don't want to run and sweat. But I also felt like it might be more symbolic than just that. On the outside, I run around all day and I go for runs, but here, I feel like I need to slow down.

I bundle up. I don't have gloves with me, so I put two pairs of socks over my hands. That's an old runner's trick. I know that 2,000 steps is roughly the equivalent of a mile, so I count my steps when I walk. It was 1,655 going down but, for some reason, 1,705 coming back up—3,360 altogether. So up and down was actually about 1.7 miles. If I do it six times a day, it's over 10 miles. That's my new goal, to walk 120 miles up and down the driveway before I leave.

After supper I lie in bed thinking. I keep wondering what I'd be doing if I was home. I'd probably be giving the kids a bath and putting them in bed. After that, I'd be lying on the couch watching the NCAA tourney and hanging out with Sara. It sounds nice.

I had another failed meditation session tonight.

Maybe I should leave soon.

Yes, you should, Billy the Bully answers.

Maybe I should have gone to the South of France to live with Thich.

I wonder what Thich is doing right now?

There's a sliver of moonlight slicing into the empty darkness of my room. Dogs are barking. The breeding house is 100 yards away, and they sound like they're right outside of my room. Lenny is only ten feet away from me. Hold on a second.

Okay I'm back. I got up out of bed and tiptoed across the room and propped a chair under the door handle. Just in case. You can never be too safe. What if Lenny is pissed that he's picking up dog shit and I'm just a distractor in training sessions? I'm starting to freak myself out a little bit.

But Lenny the Intern doesn't know something about me. No one here does.

One night in January of 2004 I was channel-surfing when I saw a late-night infomercial for a self-defense course. They were offering a package to instruct people on defending themselves. The commercial was pretty cheesy. A guy walks into a bar and six guys jump him for no apparent reason. Don't you hate when that happens? Anyway, there were a lot of swinging pool cues and crashing beer bottles. The self-defense hero jumps into action like in a vintage kung fu star. It's just like the movies when he knocks out the six roughnecks with karate chops and kicks to the head. Then he looks into the TV camera and says: "You can learn to do this, too."

I was sold.

The next day in my office, I asked Mark Orsini, a great friend of mine who was interning at Marquis Jet, to help find me the best self-defense guy in New York City. My business partner and I had started a private jet card company, so today's task was a bit unusual. For the last five weeks Mark had been checking flight times and weather patterns.

"I'm going to become a black belt in something," I told him.

The following day when I got to the office, Orsini had ten pictures with bios pinned up to a bulletin board like mug shots—it looked like a scene out of *Homeland*. He was a black belt in interning—the kid knew how to get shit done. As I looked through the pictures, Orsini said, "These guys are all hardcore, but none of them is your guy. THIS IS YOUR GUY." He held up a photo of Tim Gowdie in his hand. "He teaches Krav Maga at John Jay College of Criminal Justice."

I knew that Krav Maga is a self-defense discipline developed by the Israeli military.

"Get him on the line," I said.

After a brief call, I hired Gowdie to teach me self-defense. He's built like a wrecking ball: round, strong, and dented. I had the feeling that if I punched him in the nose, I'd break my hand. Gowdie came to my place twice a week for an hour and a half every week for a year to train. We cleared out all of the furniture in my apartment and turned my living room into an octagon. It was super intense—one day he accidentally cracked my ribs.

The checklist behind a Krav Maga first strike boils down to three basic elements: One, has someone violated your space? Two, is there a direct threat? And, three, get them before they get you. Sounds reasonable—right?

During the months that followed, I practiced all the time. I went into work and told the people in my office to put me in a bear hug to see if I could escape, to try to poke me in the eye to see if I could block it, and to throw punches at me to see if I could defend and attack. It became sort of like the Cato scenes in the Pink Panther movies—someone would jump out of the closet at me at odd moments. I wanted to see if this shit really worked. After months of training, I was ready.

I was almost looking for a confrontation to happen.

One Friday morning I was leaving my apartment in a suit and tie for an important business meeting. I never wore a suit and tie, but on this day I had to—so I was. I was also holding two trays of fruit—one in each hand—that I got at Fairway the night before to bring to the meeting. And I had a string bag over my shoulder. When I stepped onto the elevator there were two maintenance guys in there. I had lived in the building for ten years and basically knew everybody who lived and worked there. I talked to these guys all the time about the Knicks or whatever. "What's up," I said when I got on.

The elevator stopped on the next floor below us, and into the elevator walked a guy in his late twenties. I'd never seen him before, but he had this party-frat-bro-chief-big-guy look to him. And an attitude to match. It was December, but he was sweating like a faucet and his hair was all messed up. His eyes had a sheen. I moved back and over to my right to give him some room. He turned and faced the doors immediately, standing right in the middle of the elevator. But when the elevator door closed, he started backing up until he was right on top of me. I mean his back was pushing up on my fruit trays. And he kept maneuvering like an annoyed person who keeps turning their neck at the movie theater.

"Can you at least give me some room, ASSHOLE," he said.

I wasn't even sure he was talking to me at first.

"Excuse me?" I said.

He turned, looked at me, and gave a "try and fuck with me" look with red, runny eyes.

"I said give me some room, fucko," he said.

I looked at Angel, one of the maintenance guys, and he slowly shook his head as if to say, "Man, don't let him talk to you like that." The elevator started heading down. Five, four, three, two, one, the elevator doors opened. And the guy walked out.

"Maybe it's your mother's fault," he said, under his breath, but loud enough for me to hear. "The way she raised you."

I was standing there on fire. I could feel the heat rising in my body.

"What did you say?" I said.

He flipped me off as he headed for the door.

I couldn't take it anymore.

"Get the fuck over here and say it to my face," I said.

At another time in my life I would have been a little surprised and might have had some butterflies, but I was $16,000 into my Krav Maga lessons. I was dying to know if all the training worked.

But I was also holding the two trays of cantaloupe chunks and sliced bananas and wearing a suit.

Next thing I know we were nose to nose. His breath stunk of last night's vodka and who knows what. I went through my Krav Maga checklist: Is he in my space? Check. Do I feel threatened? Check. Does this guy realize I'm going to knee him so hard in the nuts that his nuts are about to be in his ears? I'd done it with my instructor 6,000 times. And then I was going to take my fruit trays and play them like cymbals on his head.

He must have sensed something because he turned quickly and left in a huff. Before I could make a move he was gone from the building, but it was like he was walking away thinking he had won.

When I got to work after my breakfast meeting I was still steaming, and I couldn't think straight. I kept replaying the scenario in my head. What should or could I have done differently? I was in the conference room, and I told everyone the story I just told you.

And they were all like, "You wimp, you let him go? The Krav Maga man!"

I was so mad. I got back in a cab and returned to my building looking for him. I don't even know why because I'd seen the guy leave, but I was so angry I wasn't thinking straight. I filled out some paperwork with the doorman to let him know the incident occurred. This way when I saw the kid again it'd be on the record that we had an argument and he instigated it. Maybe he wouldn't be able to sue me if we have a future fight, I thought.

Every single day after that I waited in the lobby for an extra beat in hopes that I'd see him again. In fact, Gowdie decided to hold one class in the elevator to simulate what might happen if the situation repeated itself. I became a master of elevator combat, using leverage against the wall, my spacing, everything. I knew every inch of that elevator.

A month goes by, then two, and there was no sign of this asshole. I wore Krav Maga sweatshirts around the building like a motorcycle gang member wears his colors—maybe I could get the word out. Okay, now that sounds a little ridiculous, but I wanted a rematch. Still there was no sight of him. I tried to time my morning elevator rides to sync with the time of the incident, but I never saw him—ever. I was starting to question if the guy even lived in the building.

Then one day, six months later, I was going for a bike ride. I pushed the elevator button and there he was, alone in the elevator at last. I was holding my bike instead of my fruit trays. I was in my slippery bike shoes—they're like wearing clogs on an ice skating rink. I was wearing my stretchy bike shorts and a stretchy bike shirt; I looked like a Frenchman in Texas. And I had my helmet on. Shit, I didn't train to fight in this outfit.

But before I could say a word, he said, "I've been hoping to run into you. I want to apologize for that last time we were on the elevator. I couldn't have been more of a dick. I was high and shit. Please forgive me."

It was like I threw sixteen grand out the window. But today's service reminded me about the importance of forgiveness. Maybe I should be thinking more about Lenny's circumstances and what makes him like that instead of being annoyed and pissed off by him. I mean, my default button is usually to flip right to annoyed.

When I get pissed off at someone who cuts me off, Sara always says, "What if that person is headed to the hospital for an emergency?" and "What if they have had a terrible day?"

She's always giving others the benefit of the doubt. It frees her from getting angry herself.

"You don't have to own it. That's their stuff," she likes to remind me.

And she's right. With all that said though, I'm still ready to kick Lenny's ass if I need to.

Okay fine, I still have a lot more work to do up here.

Meal time at the monastery.

DAY 5

The Retreat

"If you realize that all things change, there is nothing you will try and hold on to."
—LAO TZU, *DAO DE JING*

Outside of my window, I scanned the parking lot. It was starting to fill up with non-monks. An old 1970 Pontiac chugged up the driveway. Two elderly folks got out. I kept watching until they disappeared into the church; it has only been five days, but it was strange to see civilians. And then more cars drove up the driveway. And then four older folks got out. The monks had what they called a retreat today, and it didn't exactly draw a tailgate crowd.

The church was sold out. I wouldn't be surprised if there were scalpers outside of it saying, "I got two in the third pew; two in the third pew." Luckily I hustled over there early and was able to get my usual seat, but, man, that place was packed. And as a result, the church smells of monk and incense were magnified. I mean the odor of incense was everywhere. The monks burn it as both a religious ritual and a way to mask body odor or, rather, that's the original purpose of incense, I'm told.

I sat there waiting for the services and inhaled a huge whiff of incense. As soon as it hit my nose, I got an olfactory flashback to a dance crew called Soul Brothers. And there I went again with my mind—taking the scenic route to nowhere. Anyway, I toured with them in the early 1990s when my record came out.

The Soul Brothers were three guys from Los Angeles who danced for my label mate Def Jef. They had appeared on the TV show *In Living Color* and had insane street cred. When I kicked off a college tour I asked Jef if they could roll with me as my dancers to fire up the crowd. They were cool cats who loved to smoke weed. Let me put it this way—if there was such a thing as the Snoop Dogg Marijuana Olympics, these guys would win the gold medal. They knew what they were doing and burned a lot of incense to try to hide the smell.

A few years after I retired from rapping (uh-hem, I didn't get signed for a second album), I got a call from the Soul Brothers. They were going to Washington, D.C., for the Million Man March and were going to swing through New York City on their way back to Cali. They needed a place to stay and asked if they could crash at my apartment for one night. Of course, I said.

They showed up on a Monday right before I was heading to work, so I told them to make themselves at home. I think they took that literally because when I got back from work they had taken all of my family pictures off the wall and replaced them with photos of Bob Marley and Malcolm X. I could smell the incense they burned for a week.

Today the church was buzzing with anticipation. I pulled myself back from my Soul Brother reminiscences and focused on being present. There were people from all over the country for the one-day retreat. They all seemed to be searching for something we all want: happiness, meaning, and spirituality. You could just feel it in the air. I tried to get comfortable in my seat.

The festivities started off with a lecture by Sister Rebecca. She's one of three New Skete nuns. The nuns live down the mountain. They're like sorority sisters to the monks. They attend all the services and share in virtually all of the retreats, events, and functions.

The nuns came to New Skete a few years after the monks did. Their story is similar. Originally, there were a half dozen or so in a convent in Indiana, and they went looking for something a little more extreme, like a monastery on a mountain. They heard about the New Skete monks, so they came here and stayed. They've also gained some fame with the way they support themselves. They bake cheesecakes and sell them all over the world. At least that's what the word on the street, or the mountain, is.

Sister Rebecca stood at the podium at the front of the church. She looks like Aunt Bee from *The Andy Griffith Show*. Like Aunt Bee, she has mad spunk. As soon as she started talking I got drawn in—her message resonated. "Treat yourself gently. Don't talk angry to yourself. We're all searching for peace," she said. "But peace is already within. We simply need to work on our spirit."

She was explaining how we need to recognize emotions and feelings of fear. I immediately thought of Lenny. Damn him! Maybe HE is my lesson. Maybe the monks planted him here as a distraction. But thankfully Sister Rebecca reeled me back in with her words. And from there I started connecting the dots... sometimes we get lost emotionally. So that makes awareness and mindfulness like the GPS. *If we're aware of how we're feeling, it helps us process emotion to make better decisions— it gives us direction.* To me awareness isn't the same thing as gut. Gut, instinct, and educated guesses can help guide us forward, but being aware will rein in the emotional side of decision making if, and only if, we are accepting of our feelings.

If we can work gut and awareness at the same time— magic can happen.

And then at one point I looked up and Brother Gregory was standing right in front of me. He handed me a basket of what looked like Wonder Bread. I smiled and sort of put my hand up indicating a no-thank-you for the snack. I wasn't hungry. And besides it was before noon, so I can only have fruit. Brother Gregory leaned down real close to my ear...

"It was blessed at last night's vigil," he said.

I quickly grabbed one and popped it in.

Tasted like Wonder Bread to me. I grew up on the stuff.

At that point I think I was supposed to reflect on Christ's sacrifice and look forward to his return. And I have to say as far as sacrifices go—his was pretty epic. His entire life sounds like a sacrifice. It's rather ironic because it seems like today most people try to avoid sacrifices.

It was a great service this morning—loved the message and the blessed bread spoke to me as a symbol of being welcome as I am.

As we all left the church we started to get bottlenecked at the entrance; sixty people or so standing in and around the church. It was like a receiving line after a wedding ceremony. Just as I squeezed outside, one of the guests came up and gave me a big-ass bear hug. He did it on sneak attack. And it was a hug like I'd just gotten back from war.

They attracted some interesting people to the retreat, and this guy was par for the course. He was about six foot two, an

African American fellow, bubbly and seemingly high on life. But the guy was basically spooning me standing up. There was no escape.

"Brother Christopher, are you wearing new cologne?" he asked, taking a big whiff of my neck.

"Oh I'm so sorry, you have me mistaken. I'm not Brother Christopher, I'm just Jesse," I said. "And I'm not wearing any colog—"

"Just Jesse! Ahhh, the new monk!"

And then that's when he kissed me.

He planted one right on my cheek—sound effects and all. He didn't stop there. He whisked his lips around to the other cheek and kissed it again. But this was no European double-cheek air kiss. NOPE—this was the real-deal double-cheek kiss. He pulled me back from his kiss, or should I say our kiss—no, I think his kiss is more accurate—and he was still holding onto my shoulders. My cheeks must have had wet stains. And that's when I explained I wasn't a monk. But he didn't seem to care.

"Funky up here, isn't it, Just Jesse? The vibes, the air, the smells!"

The smells?

"Just Jesse, walk with me, vibe with me, and smell with me," he said.

How could I say no to that?

We walked by my room, and he stopped. And then he sniffed.

"You smell that?"

"What?"

"Orange peels. I've never smelled that up here before. There's something brewing. Can't you just smell it."

What the fuck? Does this guy have supersensory smell?

"We get some distinct smells up here if we allow ourselves to breathe, Just Jesse."

Now I was thinking maybe you can get some unique super smelling powers from being around the dogs or something. We walked over to the dining room together.

"Our time has ended, Just Jesse," he said as he found a seat.

Nice guy, but I wasn't wearing cologne.

Breakfast was silent again. It reminded me of car trips with my parents when I was young. "The first one to talk loses," Mom would declare. Every time I'd yell as loud as I could, "I LOSE!"

I didn't think that was appropriate today, so I just decided to lay low.

I met Brother Peter at lunch (sorry, dinner). He's the monk who lives in an assisted living center but comes to the monastery for some events and services. The monks told me he was "quite the talker." So I tried to steer clear. I was warned if he said, "Come spend some time with me," that meant I could be in for a few hours of conversation. And of Course . . .

I got sucked right into the reading room where we sat facing each other after lunch. Brother Peter is probably approaching eighty, but he looks like he's in his early sixties. That's a theme with the monks here; they all have a real youthfulness to them. As I get older that's the one thing I want to hold on to—youth. I recognize we can't trick time, but if we act young, think young, and play young, it can have an effect on how we deal with aging—it slows it down.

"Ahhh, Jesse. I've heard a lot about you. We haven't gotten the chance to acquaint."

"Good to meet you, Brother Pe—"

"It's interesting that a fellow with your background would be interested in our life."

"Well, I thought that—"

"What are some of your goals? What draws you to the monastic life? When I was deciding if this life was for me it was a different time. A much different time. Things were different back then. **But you know what doesn't change, Jesse? The heart. It's the heart that doesn't change. But times change. Yes, they do, but the heart remains the same if we allow it to."**

If you ask me, I'd say he's still got his wits about him.

"Well, you see," I said.

"Let me tell you a little about the monastery."

"Thanks, I think I have to—"

"It's important that we acquaint in the event you decide to make this a career path."

Career path?

"Pull up a chair, come spend some time with me..."

Fortunately, we got interrupted as those words came out of his mouth; a car was stuck in the snow, and they needed an extra body to push it forward. I ran to my room, grabbed a coat, and bundled up. When I got out there Lenny the Intern was behind the car pushing with no gloves or jacket. He looked at me with a "you lived with a Navy SEAL and you had to go get a jacket on" type of look. I think this asshole is intentionally trying to make me look bad. Like we're in some kind of private intern competition or something and he's the only one playing. I swear I'm trying to move past these negative thoughts and embrace Lenny for who he is, BUT...

I'M NOT EVEN AN INTERN.

After we freed the car from the snowbank, I got pulled into the kitchen. Brother Gregory told me I was in charge of cleaning the dishes. All 300 of them from the retreat. The monks cleared out and left me with the plates, pots, and utensils. It was like I was the rookie on a sports team who was in charge of the laundry after practice. Can't wait to tell Sara.

SARA: "What did you do at the monastery, honey?"
ME: "Dishes, dog distractor. Oh, and I walked up and
      down the hill for hours."

And while I was scrubbing a pot for the second time because it didn't pass Brother Gregory's inspection (I'm not even joking when I say I scrubbed it like a champ the first time), I overheard someone say, "Plenty have missed heaven by eighteen inches—the distance between the head and the heart."

I like that.

So I treated every plate like it was a push-up, every pot like a pull-up, and every utensil like a sit-up. I was trying to bang them out as fast as I could—harder—faster. I was crushing those dishes. And when I finally finished Brother Gregory told me it was officially my job to do the dishes for the rest of my stay.

Brother Christopher led the retreat in the afternoon. We were in the church, and he started with twenty minutes of silent meditation. I find it's easier to meditate with a room full of people. I'm not sure why. And then Brother Christopher talked about the pressure we put on ourselves to succeed.

"We spend so much time worrying about things that may never happen," he said.

And then he shifted his discussion to suffering, and that really got my attention. He said adversity is the great activator of spiritual awakenings. Suffering is the great accelerator to going inward. In the presence of dying we discover our deepest life. Death, sickness, and loss pull us into a new moment and new way of thinking. When you deal with tragedy and it doesn't rob you of joy and peace—it's a great gift for others. I have to say for someone who doesn't go deep—that's some deep shit.

I've learned a lot about myself when I suffer. But my kind of suffering doesn't compare to what Brother Christopher was talking about. My suffering has always been self-inflicted through endurance races. In 2006 I entered the USA National Ultra-marathon Championship. I adjusted my goal from winning the race to just completing the 100 miles in less than twenty-four hours. I raised money during my training and received over $1 million in donations, which only increased the pressure to finish!

I gave myself 90 days to train. And I trained like a machine. *I always tell people that when you have a BIG goal, the work necessary to accomplish it has to become an obsession. It has to become a part of your daily lifestyle and remain that way for the duration of the goal.* With that mind-set, I trained twice a day every day. It was an obsession. At night I did research, reading articles and watching videos about achieving goals. Most of what I found had the same five themes:

1) Have a specific date for your goal
2) Have an accountability partner
3) Put the goal in writing
4) Have a detailed plan to accomplishing your goal
5) Execute your plan

The research helped me maintain my obsession, but ALL of that knowledge went out the window at mile 75. My ankles were swollen to the size of grapefruits, there were six toenails floating around my socks, and blisters appeared on my feet that looked like the purple grapes you can find at Whole Foods in the produce section. In that moment I could have had "my goal" tattooed to my forehead and it wouldn't have helped me. F#ck those goals, blogs, and self-help videos; they weren't going to run the last twenty-five miles.

As I tried to keep running on the 1.1-mile dirt loop in Grapevine, Texas, I was struggling. But the short loop provided an opportunity for me to see the other runners during the race. And one of those runners competing was Pam Reed, a legend in the world of ultra-running. She's famous for not only completing the Badwater race (the hardest race in the word) but winning it. As Pam passed me we started to chat. Well, as much as one can chat while running their seventy-sixth mile.

"I'm not feeling it today," she said. "This is my last lap. I'm going home."

NO!

I explained to Pam I was running for charity and needed her help. I knew she could provide a wealth of information when the shit hit the fan. And truth be told—the shit was already flying around—I was in trouble. But I knew she'd seen it all. I needed her with me for the balance of the race to "coach" me through the pain. Thankfully she agreed with a smile.

"Just keep moving," she said. "Block it out of your mind. It's not going to kill you. Keep moving forward. Don't stop."

I listened to her. I kept moving—one leg at a time—loop after loop.

"The pain will last a week," Pam told me. "But you'll have the memory forever."

At mile 84 she saw the self-doubt creeping back into my bones. My legs were like Jell-O, and I truly wasn't sure if I could finish. I wanted to quit. She looked me in the eye as I was about to utter the words: *I don't know if I can make it.*

"No matter what," she said. "Keep advancing."

I crossed the finish line twenty-two hours and thirty minutes after the race started. It landed me in a wheelchair for three days, but I finished! I'd have never made it without Pam's advice, guidance, and support along the way. And that experience of suffering has helped me in so many other facets of my life. The memory has helped me cross many other finish lines. And I know that isn't the kind of suffering Brother Christopher was talking about, but what he said makes a lot of sense to me. I get it. Suffering can give us power.

DAY 6
Mr. Sara Blakely

"When it is obvious that the goals cannot be reached, don't adjust the goals, adjust the action steps."
— CONFUCIUS

When you're alone for an extended period of time all the concerns around work, schedule, and people you're pissed off at go away, and the important things rise to the front of your mind. I really miss my kids. And of course I miss my wife. Just thinking about her reminds me of a few nights before I left.

I headed over to a restaurant called 10 Degrees South with my friend and trainer, Marq. We were meeting Sara there. The three of us planned to have a nice dinner while my kids were with my parents. We love the restaurant—the food and décor are South African, which make it a fun and tasty place to go. And it's not far from our house. It's in Buckhead just off of Roswell Road.

When Marq and I walked in we saw Justin. He and his wife own the place. Justin is an ex-professional soccer player who's got gorilla strength. And when he saw us he ran over to pull me into his clutches. He squeezed me like my son Lazer squeezes the toothpaste. There's nothing gentle about it. My guess is he's broken numerous ribs with that hugging technique. After our gorilla greeting he walked us through the bungalow-inspired dining room over to the indoor patio. We sat down and waited for our waiter.

And then I felt it.

You know that feeling when you can just tell someone is looking at you—yeah, that feeling—I had it. Eyes were on me like a heat-seeking missile. I looked up from the menu and scanned the dining room. There she was. A woman, perhaps a recent college grad, was laser focused on me. She had wavy blonde hair, a pair of slender tan legs, and piercing blue eyes—staring. I quickly turned away, trying to play it off like I was looking for Justin or something.

I looked over at Marq to see if he saw what I saw, but he was reading his menu. He was in his own little world. I kicked him under the table.

"Marq," I said like a ventriloquist. "Table 12."

"You think I know the table numbers?"

"Whatever you do—don't look now, but over there," I said. "I think she's checking me out."

"Who? Where?"

I gave him the slightest nod with my head and guided him to the location with my eyes. Marq turned his chair around like he was positioning himself to see a performance of *Hamilton*. He definitely would fail as a private investigator—so blatant. And then he quickly turned back around when he got caught in the act. And this young lady kept her eyes on me the entire time.

She wouldn't quit.

"Did someone clone Kate Upton," Marq said. "Holy shizzzznit."

And then he whipped back around to make sure she was still looking. Oh yeah—she was.

"She is checking you out, man," he said. "Dang."

We were both baffled. Every time I looked up she was still staring. This woman was like the antithesis of Medusa—instead of turning people to stone she could turn them into Jell-O. Her stare went on for an hour; okay fine, I lied, but it was like three very, very, very long minutes. I must say it felt good to be checked out by such an attractive female. I guess that's what it feels like to be swiped right in public. And when you're forty-eight years old, you've got to take what you can get.

It was a nice ego boost—harmless, but nice.

And then she stood up and started walking toward our table. Her eyes were still laser focused but now accompanied by a huge friendly Georgian smile. This is bananas, I thought to myself. What is she doing? What if she propositions me? What if Sara walks in when I'm just chatting her up? Should I not talk to her? But isn't that rude? She got closer and closer until she was standing right next to our table.

Marq grabbed his water and quickly filled his mouth with it.

"Excuse me," the young lady said. "I'm so sorry to interrupt. But can I ask you a question?"

"SURE! I mean, sure."

And then she paused for a moment.

"Are you? Are you married to Sara Blakely?"

WHAT?

Marq's water squirted out the sides of his mouth and then he covered it with a napkin.

"Um yeah," I said. "I am."

"Oh my God," she said. "I love her. I love what she does. She's such an inspiration. Oh my god, I can't believe it. I can't believe you're Sara Blakely's husband."

"Yup. That's me."

I thanked her for the kind words about my wife and told her that Sara would have loved meeting her. She gushed a few more times before telling us that she had to run to meet her friends at some club called Sanctuary. She didn't even drop an invite—so rude. And then just like that she was gone. Marq busted out laughing.

"Fuck off," I said.

The reality is I'm very comfortable having a wife who's in the public eye. I could see how that could generate a lot of insecurity, but I take a lot of pride in being Sara's biggest fan and cheerleader. Sure, there are times when it feels weird to sit at a dinner event where everyone wants to talk to Sara way more than me, but it's fun to watch her star shine bright. That's what teamwork is all about.

A big part of marriage is sharing in each other's successes. And I picked a great teammate.

About ten minutes later, Sara walked through the door. I immediately told her about what had happened with the woman checking me out. She thought it was hysterical. And then our waiter stopped by to fill Sara's water and told us about the specials.

I love the food there, but I always consider it a cheat day. Sara, on the other hand, thinks it's her healthy meal of the week. There have been many nights when I've seen her take down an entire box of Cheez-Its for dinner. She defines healthy as the plate having something green on it—like a sauce.

When we were ready Sara ordered sweet ground beef curry topped with savory custard; Marq went with the eighteen-ounce bone-in ribeye, and I got butternut squash ravioli. As we waited for our food to be delivered, we talked about the topic on all of our minds. What was I going to do at a monastery?

The three of us kept chatting until our food came.

After we finished up the waiter stopped by and offered some dessert.

Justin's mom makes the desserts—they're called Di-Delights. And everything she makes is fantastic. We've never had a bad one. They're INSANELY good. The waiter asked Marq and me if we wanted anything, but we passed because we were planning to get a run in later.

"I'll have the fruit cake," Sara said with a smile.

"You're splurging," I said. "I love it."

"Splurging? What are you talking about?"

"That thing is going to have like 18,000 calories."

"Eighteen thousand calories of fun," she said. "Plus it has fruit in it, silly. It's healthy."

God I love my wife.

I've learned so much from being around Sara. That's another reason I miss her so much. She makes me better—at everything. I feel like we're Karl Malone and John Stockton to each other. They were two skilled professional basketball players who made each other's game better. They played knowing each other's strengths and weaknesses and used it to their advantage. Sometimes I'm the point guard giving her an assist, and other times she's passing the ball to me down low so I can score.

And sometimes we're Thelma and Louise, except we don't drive off of cliffs.

But one of the things I love most about Sara is her story and determination.

Growing up, Sara always wanted to be a lawyer, but she failed the LSATs...twice. So instead of heading to law school after college, she decided to go to Disney World and try out to be Goofy...of course she did! When she arrived she was too short for the job (minimum height is five feet eight and Sara is five feet six) so they asked her to be a chipmunk instead.

After a short stint at Disney, Sara accepted a job with an office supply company called Danka and sold fax machines door to door...for seven years. One night before heading out for a party, she didn't like the way her own butt looked in white pants. She took a pair of scissors and cut off the feet of her pantyhose to avoid panty lines and have a smoother look under her clothes. Voilà, her invention and big idea was born.

Still, having a big idea and turning it into a big reality isn't nearly the same thing. Here's where having experience can be a dream-crusher. People have great ideas all the time, but they have just enough experience, and have seen just enough failure, to start to believe their chances of failing are too high.

Sara didn't know enough to think her chances of succeeding were low. Besides, failure was never a big thing for her. *At the dinner table growing up, Sara's father had a weekly ritual where he would ask her what she failed at that week.* Maybe she had tried out for the school play, cheerleading, or a sports team. When she'd tell her dad how poorly it went, he would give her a high five. Whether she had succeeded or failed wasn't important. All that mattered was that she tried. *That ritual changed Sara's definition of failure, and failure became tied to not trying rather than the outcome.*

Over the course of the next two years selling fax machines, Sara worked on developing her new idea after work, at night, and on the weekends. She took $5,000 she had set aside in savings to start the company. Since she had never taken a business class, she operated on instinct and gut.

Instead of using her entire budget on legal fees to patent her product, Sara bought a book on patents and wrote her own patent. She used bold colors in her packaging to make her products pop off the shelves. She spent twelve hours a day in department stores promoting her products for two straight years. It worked!

The name Spanx came to Sara while sitting in traffic in Atlanta. She knew that Kodak and Coca-Cola were two of the most recognized brands in the world and that both names shared a strong "k" sound. She figured it must be good luck. She changed the "ks" to an "x" at the last minute because she heard that made-up words are easier to trademark than real words.

When she launched her product she began cold-calling buyers in department store chains and got nowhere. She eventually got a meeting at Neiman Marcus in Dallas, but her sales pitch wasn't going so well. So Sara called an audible and asked the buyer to follow her into the bathroom. This was a first for the buyer, but she was a good sport. Sara put the footless pantyhose on in the bathroom and did her own "before and after." The buyer said, "I get it. I'll try them in seven stores!"

Today, Spanx has expanded way beyond just the shapewear that made them famous. They now have a cult following for their leggings, activewear, swimwear, bras, apparel, and her latest invention—arm tights. Sara somehow just knows what customers want. It's fun to watch. She is an inventor at heart and holds several patents. But what she is most proud of is Spanx's greater mission of elevating women.

Regardless, what I miss most about her is her unconditional love for her family, friends, and children.

I went to check out the library this afternoon, and as I headed back to my room, I had to pass the kitchen to get there. And I spotted a jar filled with chocolate Clif Bars. Josh the Cook must have picked them up today. I used some bionic counting skills and immediately realized there were eleven bars...

One for each monk, Lenny the Intern, and me.

I was famished. The fruit and soup diet had me craving these bars.

Maybe the monks don't even know about them.

Maybe Josh just put them out.

Maybe monks don't even like Clif Bars.

All kinds of thoughts flew into my head.

And honestly my hand went into the jar to grab one, just one. But...

I sinned.

I took all eleven bars back to my room and ate three before heading out...

3:00 p.m.

Simple manual labor helps keep your mind clear, they say.

And they're right. It does. I don't mind doing the work, it's just...

I don't know. I'm having a hard time articulating my feelings.

This afternoon I scrubbed the church floors with a single scrub brush, along with Lenny the Intern, on our hands and knees. And those floors were D-I-R-T-Y. There's nothing like monk dirt with all the work boots clomping around, all of the people from the retreat, and the incense burning twice a day.

I tried talking to Lenny to plot out a strategy for the floor, but he didn't say a word. How do people do that? Just not respond. Even when I'm in a disagreement with someone...even if I'm pissed, I respond. I say something. But talking to Lenny is like speaking braille.

"Lenny, you want to start at the back and I'll start at the front?"

Nothing.

As I started cleaning I seriously wondered why I came up to the monastery in the first place. Sure, I'm learning, but time is going by so slowly. I have to start listening to my wife. Just like my mom, she's virtually always right, which makes sense because Sara is a mom too. She told me I just jump into things without thinking. And my mom used to say, "Be happy with what you have."

I should listen to both of them. But instead Billy the Bully was in attack mode.

I mean, maybe I should have just stayed with my mom for a couple of weeks instead.

I thought I was going to a monastery like the ones in Tibet. Instead, I get dog whisperers in jeans and sweatshirts. And scrub brushes. I kept grinding the bristles of the brush to the floor—hard. If I was going to be cleaning the floor, I at least wanted to do it well.

There was a point when I was scrubbing that I looked over at Lenny, who was scrubbing like his life depended on it, and said to myself: If he says one word to me, I'm going to make him eat the brush—not very monkish, but I was annoyed. I don't know why I get myself into these types of situations. I moved a Navy SEAL into my house for heaven's sake! I went to live at a monastery filled with German shepherds! What's next? Alligator wrestling? A nudist colony in Antarctica? *Dancing with the Stars*?

Why do I keep looking for something I don't have? I think it's because I don't want to miss out on life. I mean, we only get one shot at it, so why not try to create as many memories as possible?

I rolled over so I was sitting on my butt and looked up at the iconic portraits on the wall. Moses looked like you see him in most paintings, old, with a long, white beard and holding two tablets with the Ten Commandments. He seemed to be looking back at me.

"What's the matter with you?" Moses said. "Did you come all this way for nothing?"

In my ear, he talked like Jackie Mason.

"I made a mistake. I shouldn't have come."

"A mistake? So that's the lesson you're going home with? Never go to a monastery?"

"Something like that."

"Don't be a putz," Moses said. "The lesson is in your hand."

"There's nothing in my hand but this stupid brush."

"Exactly."

While I was looking at the brush, the realization hit me like a Jackie Chan kung fu kick to the side of my head. The fact I wasn't being tested by the monks was a test in itself. This wasn't supposed to be some magical spiritual journey. I wasn't supposed to levitate or reach enlightenment. I was supposed to scrub the floor and wash the dishes. I was supposed to learn by being a part of the community and by doing what they do.

Billy the Bully faded away.

It was in that moment I shifted gears and understood that sometimes we're just supposed to experience things; to allow them to happen naturally and be present for the moment. Stop worrying about things like whether my son scores at his soccer game...and just appreciate the fact he's healthy enough to be in the game. Floor scrubbing took three hours. And I must say it looked fantastic when we were finally done, like the ice at Madison Square Garden right after the Zamboni finishes making its rounds between the first and second period. I'm proud of the job we did.

I stood there for a moment admiring our work. It felt good. I felt good.

Afterward I took a walk and did some soul-searching. I'm here for the experience, I told myself, and I have to remember that. I'll never get another opportunity to give myself an extended time-out and live at a monastery. I reminded myself of the two types of moments (the ones we can't control and the ones we create) and started to celebrate the fact that I'm creating this memory. So I need to focus. I'm going to try to absorb everything I can from the monks by participating, observing, and really trying to get to know them. I'm going to try to be part of the community as much as I can. I'll try to have fun too.

I need to be strategic about this—I'm going to try to find out everything I can about this place and somehow figure out how to stop the noise in my head. Just because I'm staying in one of the quietest places on earth doesn't mean the noise between the ears stops. It seems like mine never stops.

The idea of going home early still has some oxygen.

The internal enemy is alive. The bully in my head. He still whispers to me: "It's time to go..."

At the evening service the Clif Bars got their revenge. My stomach was like an overstuffed washing machine on full tilt. It was growling so loudly and I could feel everyone in the congregation looking at me. I should have known a monastery is the wrong place to mess with karma. I'm sorry.

11:00 p.m.

About two hours ago, I think it was 9:00 p.m., I went with Brother Stravros to clean the dog pens. Every night he walks to the training center to let the dogs run outside so he can clean. Tonight he asked me to join him. It was FREEZING and pitch black out as we walked the 200 yards from our sleeping quarters. Stavros didn't bring a flashlight. He navigated the trail like it was the middle of a sunny day. No issues. SEAL would love this guy.

"I can clean the pens, if you want to play with the dogs," I said.

"Nah," he said. "You should get to enjoy the dogs. Connect with them."

"Great."

I was instructed during my time as a distractor to always greet a dog in a nonthreatening position, with your hands low to the ground making a fist. So when one of the dogs came over to greet me, I did just that. Not only does that calm the dog, but there's less flesh on your knuckles in the event you get bitten.

As soon as the dog reached me, she bypassed my fist and made a mad dash for my nuts. One of the side effects of being up here alone is it has made me super horny. I think the dogs are picking up on it because she stuck her nose in my groin and sniffed me like a security dog checking for bags of cocaine at the airport. Stavros pulled her back and instructed me to hand her a treat. I did. She gobbled it in one bite; better a treat than my nuts. And then she took one last whiff before Stavros put her back in the crate.

I'd already had my fill of dogs this evening after the first one, but we stayed with them until about 10:15 p.m. and then headed back. When I got to our building, I saw Lenny's door slightly open and heard some chanting coming from his room. I tiptoed into my room and wedged the meditation chair under my door handle to create a homemade lock. I'm not going to let anyone get me up here.

DAY 7

I Didn't Learn This in College

"An ounce of practice is worth more than tons of preaching."

—MAHATMA GANDHI

I was talking to some of the monks today about happiness again. But they were really trying to get my perspective. They wanted to know what I thought. I said something like: I believe happiness is a totally pure emotion. They were curious what I meant, so I told them two stories.

It was 1985, and I was on the couch in my living room hanging out with my friend Myron. He was part of my crew—a two-man break-dancing crew. We got together every weekend and performed our routine wherever we could. One day I said to him, "Let's go to Washington, D.C., and perform on the street. There's no way those kids are as good as us."

And it was true, kids in other parts of the country were at least six months behind people breaking in New York—this is where shit was invented. So there was no way they'd be better than us. By the time other kids saw stuff on MTV, we were already on to the next.

The idea had come out of nowhere, but like most good ideas, those are the ones to jump on. So we convinced my older sister Jill, who had recently gotten her license, to drive us down there. All we had to do was offer to pay her for a ride and her silence—under no circumstances could she tell Mom. She liked the plan. So the next morning at 7:00 a.m. we piled into her car and hit the road.

Break-dancing had become my full-fledged passion by my sophomore year of high school. I used to record shows like *Soul Train* and movies like *Flashdance* and try to learn every move. I'd watch in slow motion on my VCR and practice in front of a mirror. Even my parents supported it. How many parents would let their son empty out the garage and fill it with cardboard boxes, a boom box, and mirrors to practice break-dancing instead of putting their cars in there? My parents were cool with it, but I couldn't tell them we were on our way to D.C.

While my sister drove, Myron and I strategized on how we'd perform our routine. We kept trying to perfect the plan and come up with other ideas to make our act even better. We also had to navigate; we had maps and my dad's road atlas to help figure out the best routes, but with each mile doubt started to creep into our minds. What if nobody shows up? What if we suck? What if people laugh at us? And eventually six hours later, we completed the four-hour journey.

We were nervous as hell, but it was too late to back out.

We found a parking lot next to a bank in Georgetown and set up shop. We had a huge boom box and mix tapes that we recorded off the radio—commercial breaks and all—and then we hit play. We started doing our three-minute routine. But like I said, we didn't think the plan out too much because once the first three minutes were up, we weren't sure what to do next.

So, I'd do my thing and point to Myron. And then he'd do his thing and point to me. And then I'd do my thing and point to him. You can tell where this is going…but then a crowd started to form as we danced. After thirty minutes or so I took off my hat and passed it around. The money started to pile up.

When we were done we took a ten-minute break and then started up again. And eventually a new crowd would come and watch. We kept doing it—all day. My sister just stayed there and watched; she was part of every crowd. Eventually, though, we got kicked out by the manager of the bank. He said we weren't allowed to be doing this in the parking lot.

We collected $280 that day. And after we paid my sister her fee, gave her gas money, and bought lunch, we were left with $82. It was almost all singles and change. We each earned $41. I gave Myron his cut, and he counted it out one by one. And once he was done, he came running over to me and gave me the biggest bear hug ever. "Jess! We are fucking rich," he yelled.

It was the most amazing feeling ever. I'd gotten over my fear of performing in front of people, we were doing something that we loved, and we were rich. In 1985, $41 went a long way for a teenager. We couldn't stop smiling the entire drive home—it was pure bliss. And when we pulled into our driveway back on Long Island, I looked over at my sister and thanked her again.

"How far do you think it is to drive to Texas?" I asked.

The monks really liked that story, but then I told them this one.

Fast-forward twenty-plus years: I was sitting by the pool at the Beverly Hills Hotel, and the sun was shining. I had a free day and had just ordered a big lunch. My friend Orlando and I were making plans for the evening when my phone rang. It was my

Marquis Jet partner. I picked up the call, and he told me to sit down. I was already sitting in a lounge chair.

"Warren Buffett's company wants to buy our company," he said.

Our company literally had changed the aviation business. Over the past nine years we had identified a market of people who wanted to fly privately a few times a year, clients who had the ability to purchase twenty-five hours of flight time instead of chartering a plane, signing a five-year contract, or actually owning their own jet. We had done $5 billion in sales, had hundreds of employees, and always dreamed of some day selling our company.

"Okay then," I said to my partner. "Let's do it."

We were selling our company to NetJets, part of Warren Buffett's Berkshire Hathaway. It was incredible. And then I got off the phone and looked at Orlando. I told him the news. He couldn't believe it. He was so excited for us.

When I was done telling the monks the stories, I posed this question: If you asked 1,000 people what would make me happier, (A) driving to D.C., break-dancing all day, and making $41, or (B) selling a company to NetJets/Berkshire Hathaway, what would people choose? My guess is all 1,000 people would answer B. And they'd be wrong. That day with Myron was one of the happiest of my life—a real high. The obvious lesson is that money won't bring you happiness—but everyone already knows that. For me, ***it's more about happiness being a choice. I prefer to look at happiness as a lifestyle, not a goal.***

The monks liked that—they liked it a lot.

But here's the rub. As much as I love the lifestyle that includes new challenges and adventures, if I keep seeking these out to acquire more happiness, is it problematic that the lifestyle

I live on a daily basis, the one that exists right in front of me, still needs more feeding? Happiness should never be insatiable.

So today marked my one-week anniversary here, and what I've learned is...this isn't just a monastery—it's a freaking BUSINESS SCHOOL! I got a chance to speak with the three nuns. Man, these are smart nuns. They started a cheesecake business with $1K in savings. They went to six local restaurants in the beginning and asked them to carry their cheesecakes on a trial basis. Now, they're world famous and bake 20,000 cakes a year! They make and sell them at their home and ship them all over the world. If you buy in person, the sales process works on the honor system. You walk in, nobody's there. You take a cheesecake out of the fridge, put cash in an envelope, and slide it though a slot.

As a serial entrepreneur I love the way they bootstrapped their business. The monks are amazing bootstrappers too. They have three main revenue streams: they sell about fifty puppies a year at $3,500 each, have the dog training program that allows them to house six dogs at a time, charging $2,500 per dog each session, and they smoke cheese. Cheese, I tell you!

But in addition to their primary revenue focus they also write bestselling books and have retreats on the property. And it doesn't end there; they have a marketing department, they're on social media, and they have a lovely gift shop that keeps the register ringing. Of course they also have expenses to look after, like the cook, the maintenance man, and everyday living.

But they definitely make enough money to keep the lights on. They're in the black.

It's a super-efficient operation, and young entrepreneurs could learn a lot from their infrastructure. They each have ownership of their own "division" but know the roles of the others in case they have to fill in. It works like this, one monk is in charge of each vertical:

Brother Gregory: the guests, activities, and the gift shop.
Brother Mark: kitchen and services.
Brother Thomas: dog training program.
Brother Luke, Brother John: dog breeding.
Brother Ambrose: cheese.
Brother Stavros: the church.
Brother Christopher: oversees the whole thing.

ONE TEAM, ONE DREAM. And what I love most is that they're completely self-taught. They learned all of this on the fly. No experience necessary. *I always say experience is overrated. It takes too long. Start the process and figure the rest out. If you wait too long someone else will beat you to the punch or that bully in your head will talk you out of pursuing your idea.*

I was excited by everything. So excited that I sat down with Brother Christopher to talk strategy. I had a list of ideas I thought could be moneymakers for the monastery.

"You guys are experts," I said.

Brother Christopher smiled.

"I think you have an opportunity. Since you're an authority in your industry, you can leverage that credibility and expand well beyond breeding and training. The obvious extension would be to sell leashes, collars, and dog toys, but that income is not recurring. Let's set up a line of dog food and vitamins for everyone who buys a puppy. If each dog lives on average for ten-plus years and we get them on a monthly food plan, it will add up."

I quickly took out a pen and did the math for Brother Christopher. Fifty puppies a year, multiplied by twelve months of food, multiplied by ten years, etc. It becomes quite lucrative and it never stops. This would be a great way to add an additional revenue stream for the life of EACH dog. Plus, I already have the name—"Man's Blessed Friend."

He liked that. But I knew he needed more convincing, so I told him this story. Recently, my friend in Atlanta asked me to meet with the founder of a company called KNOW Foods. He told me they make a line of grain-free, gluten-free, dairy-free, everything-free breads, pastas, waffles, and cookies that he said were delicious. He told me they were raising money and thought it'd be a fit for me, given my lifestyle.

I explained that I really don't invest in anything outside of my own projects, but after listening to my friend's hard pitch, I agreed to a meeting only. No strings. *At this stage of my life I have a very simple formula—I want low aggravation and high reward. If something has a super-high return but comes with a lot of aggravation, I'm not interested.* That goes for investments, friends, travel, EVERYTHING. So, I agreed to meet under the condition this potential investment would come with little to no aggravation. He agreed.

The founder, Steve Hanley, showed up with a bread box filled with products. Since my son eats gluten-free, I'd tried almost every gluten-free product on the market. When I bit into the sliced bread with an avocado on top, the whole notion of aggravation went away. I wanted in.

The more I learned about the product, the more I liked it. It had very few ingredients, which made it easier on your digestion. I knew all the ingredients, and it was tasty and nutritiously superior to anything I'd seen on the market. The one potential knock was there were no preservatives in the foods, which would greatly impact the shelf life of the products. This product could go bad quickly.

While everyone thought that was a big negative, I thought it was actually a big positive.

"God didn't make food to sit on a shelf in a plastic package for two years," I told Steve. "This message may actually resonate with our customers."

After our second meeting I was so impressed I moved Steve's entire team into Spanx's office. They took over the second floor and used the kitchen as their new products lab. After some diligence, it was now time to decide on the investment. I put Steve in touch with my team of advisors. I was certain they'd love this opportunity.

One of the best things I did when I could afford it was hire experts. Some of those experts sit on a small investment committee that oversees all of the deals Sara and I make. That is a serious upgrade from my old investment team...ME!

"Steve, send all the info to my team to evaluate," I said.

A day or two later I got a call from my lead dawg.

"Jesse, I have a recommendation on the KNOW Foods investment," he said.

"Great, how much do you think we should put in the deal?"

"Actually, NOTHING. I think you're NUTS to invest in this."

"Wait, what?"

"The CEO has no experience in the food business. NONE. He also has zero marketing background. I mean, he's never done anything like this. How's he going to get all the manufacturing and sales off the ground?"

He had a point, but then I asked this question: "Have you ever actually met Steve?"

"No."

"Have you seen the fire in his eyes?"

"No."

"Have you seen his passion for making this work?"

"No."

"WIRE HIM THE MONEY."

Again, you are the business plan. If I would've told someone in my twenties I was going to start a private jet company with no money, no experience in aviation, no rich friends, and no airplanes—they'd have laughed me out of the room. *If you marry your dreams with drive, urgency, passion, and a burning desire to finish what you start—you can do ANYTHING.*

I summarized my idea to Brother Christopher in two sentences: "There's reoccurring revenue for you guys while also being able to improve the dog's lives. If you find supplements that you truly believe in—they can help the dog's health—it's a win-win.

"Let's keep the lines of communication open on this," Brother Christopher said.

While I was speaking with Brother Christopher I felt pumped up, animated, and alive. It's like my words and actions were coming from another place—a pure place. These are cues I look for in myself when talking business and or ideas with other people. Just as I was clearly able to see it in Steve Hanley's eyes—I could feel it inside of me when talking with Brother Christopher.

That tells me, regardless of what I do in the future, I should stay connected to my passion.

6:00 p.m.

Sundays are "help yourself to supper" nights, which is another way of saying leftovers. Brother Christopher made pasta and left a note that read: Up for grabs. I grabbed. After dinner I watched the news with the brothers. We all huddled around a small television in the reading room. It's for Sunday evening news updates. Mostly I watched the monks watch the news.

And like all great bullies, Billy came out of nowhere. I started working up the courage to announce my plans for a departure. It sort of felt like getting psyched up to ask a girl out back in junior high; I wanted to ask her, but I didn't have the courage to say it—not out loud.

Actually, it was probably more like working up the courage to break up with a girlfriend.

But then the monks were smiling and laughing—making me feel part of the group. It was nice. And during TV time, they invited me to go on a hike with a few of them tomorrow. It felt good to be included, and I was excited to get off the monastery. But it squashed my plans of letting them know I was thinking about leaving. After the invite to hike, I couldn't tell them. Still, I'm going to book a return trip to Atlanta soon.

DAY 8
Off Campus

"In this day and age, we are dangerously out of touch with the nonhuman world around us, leaving our ears dulled and our vision blurred."
—THE MONKS OF NEW SKETE

It's hiking day, and we're going off the property.

Getting off the monastery has me fired up. We're leaving soon.

I was just in the dining room, and a couple of the brothers were getting their packs ready. Everyone was fired up. Fired up in a monk way—smiles and shit, but you could feel the energy.

"We'll leave in ten minutes," Stavros said. "Be ready."

"Roger that."

He asked if I like hiking. I told him about Mount Washington and how inspirational of a climb it was. He must have seen the excitement in my eyes because he started getting excited too. He told me they hike every Monday and how some of their climbs have been extremely grueling. This guy is seventy-plus years old. There are people half his age who think walking to the fridge is grueling. He must have some crazy monk hiking strength.

This is going to be great.

Fifteen minutes later...

I walked up to the parking area, but there was only one small car in the lot. Brother Stavros was waiting and told me to hop in the back. And then he said Lenny the Intern, Brother Mark, Brother Thomas, and Brother Thomas's dog would be there shortly.

He was kidding, right? Five adults and a huge dog in this tiny car?

He wasn't kidding. As I turned around I saw them coming up the hill. It seemed like I was the only one concerned about the amount of room in the car. We piled in. Brother Mark popped the trunk and yelled "up in the trunk" and his dog jumped right in and laid down. Brother Mark took the front seat, Lenny sat next to me in the back, and then Brother Thomas came around and in through Lenny's side. It forced Lenny into the middle. We used to call that "riding bitch" growing up. But I was pretty sure no one would find anything humorous or entertaining with me sharing that tidbit.

Lenny squished in between us in a weird yoga position.

The car was in worse shape than Turney's. Dog hair everywhere, old maps on the floor, mud all over the seats. The car looked like it hadn't been washed in years...because it hadn't been washed in years. With five grown men it didn't smell that great either. Whatever, man, I thought, we're going hiking!

Brother Stavros took off like someone just waved the green and yellow flag at the Daytona 500. GO! He flew down the driveway and accelerated into the first right turn. Maybe monks have some type of force field that keeps them from getting hurt in accidents? Last I looked, I didn't have one. But honestly, I didn't care. I was dying to get off of the monastery grounds and see some of the real world.

For the last seven days I've only been able to walk to the mobile homes and turn around.

And right on cue, the two wild dogs went bonkers as we whizzed past the mobile homes. Twenty yards later we hit the main road and the barks faded from earshot. Stavros wasn't slowing down. He went from Daytona to Le Mans down the mountainous curves. I'm exaggerating, but each time he'd take the curve in the road, Lenny the Intern, in a downward pretzel position, would slam into Brother Thomas or me.

But the only thing that mattered was we were going for a hike. And there's no way God would let a car full of monks with an intern and me get into a car crash, right? When we hit the straightaway, sort of a country route, I started absorbing the surroundings. I wanted to soak them all in. And everything was a landmark for me in case I'm able to someday run off of the property.

Stavros kept flying down the narrow road. We passed through a town that had a gas station, a school, and a Rite-Aid. And then Brother Thomas told me we were going to stop at the Rite-Aid on the way home because Lenny needed ear drops. Ear drops?

"Poor guy has been just about stone deaf for a week," he said.

Wait, he's been deaf?

Lenny the Intern is deaf?

That's what's wrong with him?

He's not a serial killer?

He just can't hear?

Holy crap! I felt bad for a moment—I'd misjudged him. But then I wondered why ear drops were the solution. The guy can't hear, and they want to get him ear drops? How about a hospital? How about before the hike? This is insanity.

"Five more minutes," Brother Stavros said at a red light. "Are you ready, Jesse?"

"Yes sir."

We finally arrived at our destination. It was called Battenkill River. Our "guide" greeted us as we arrived. His name was Bo, and I learned that Bo hikes with the monks every week. He has to be eighty years old and looks like he could be a love interest of one of the Golden Girls. But I have to give it to him—he was prepared. Bo pulled out a backpack that would put Dora the Explorer to shame. He had duct tape, purification pills, a first-aid kit, a compass, and flares.

Where were we going that we would need purification pills or flares? Oh boy.

This is going to be intense, I thought.

After we all gathered around, Bo pulled out a map to show us where we'd be hiking today. I got tiny butterflies floating around my stomach as the map unfolded. It was almost go time. And then finally he pointed at the 2.5-mile paved road on the map.

"When we get to the top of the road we'll eat here," he said. "Turn around and come home."

Wait—what? We're hiking up a paved road? I didn't say that out loud, but I was thinking it. Why did he have all of this safety stuff if we're going up and down a road? It was impossible to get lost on a paved road. What's next, a climb up an escalator?

After the initial surprise it I got over it. Enjoy the process, I told myself.

It was fairly warm out, so I packed light. I figured we'd sweat going up the mountain—I mean hill. I knew from my Mount Washington experience the importance of layering up, but I didn't think that was necessary today. We started heading up, which I figured would take a total of two hours, but about ten minutes in I realized at the pace we were going we'd be out here for five hours.

Meanwhile, Lenny the Intern took off like it was a race. It was like he's mad that I got so much attention about Mount Washington and he had something to prove. I thought about going after him and leaving the monks, but I couldn't do that.

Stav and Bo were super slow, so I rolled up with Brother Thomas, Brother Mark, and his dog. About five minutes up the hill, Brother Mark came to a stop, turned to me, and said, "Go ahead a bit and please don't look back...I have to yellow the snow here."

This gave me an opportunity for some one-on-one time with Brother Thomas. Of course I've seen him every day since training the dogs with him, but this was a great opportunity to really get to know him. He's thirty-three and the youngest of the monks. I was really curious about what he misses most. He said the freedom of saying: "Hey, I want to get Chinese food tonight."

I totally get that. I miss that too. One thing I'm struggling with is the idea of freedom. I do have freedom, but I don't really have freedom of choice up here. Many of the things I have access to at home I don't have here: a stocked fridge, a car, a microwave and bicycle. While part of me likes this simplicity, I'm also missing many comforts from home that I take for granted. I couldn't do this full time.

Like all the monks, Brother Thomas pledged all of his belongings to the monastery when he came. His only possession is a driver's license. Makes me wonder—if I'm a cop and pull a monk over for speeding, would I give him a ticket?

Brother Thomas's car and everything he owned was turned over to the monastery. Now if he wants something he goes to petty cash or for bigger purchases it goes to committee to decide if it's necessary and approved. One of the vows all the monks take is poverty, meaning the nonattachment to things. Just within their means—sounds similar to SEAL. He perfected the minimalist lifestyle. After he stayed with me, it inspired me to clean out my garage and closets to get down to thirty items. Liberating. Not a single day has gone by where I have said, *"Wow, I really wish I had a second bicycle pump!"* It de-cluttered my mind too. It freed up energy. It's like I didn't have to spend any thought on what I was going to wear that day. I just put on what was hanging in the closet. I think the monks have all of those same freedoms.

We kept climbing the hill.

The monks must take four vows:

#1 Poverty: the nonattachment to things. Just within your means.

#2 Chastity: people are expected to have matured within their sexuality. I asked Brother Stavros if he felt deprived of sex. He said he's not deprived because he chose this life.

#3 Obedience: you agree to cooperate with the order of the community. It's about respect to the moment you're in— responsibility for one another. Some communities have an abbot (where the buck stops). New Skete doesn't any longer. They have a prior, Brother Christopher, who has been voted into term. But everyone has input, and it's more by consensus or majority.

#4 Stability: "That you stay in one place"—that's why the cemetery is right there.

"Does everyone get along?" I asked.

"I'm going to live with Thomas," Stavros said behind me. "I'm committed to him and the others. Because of that commitment, why wouldn't I want to be at peace with him?"

Every Friday at 7:15 p.m. the monks have "sharing." You have five minutes to discuss anything that's on your mind with the others and what may have happened during the week. It's also a time to clear things up if you're pissed at someone. And at the end of five minutes there's a chance for the other monks to respond. That seems like a really great system to me. I made a mental note to mention this to Sara when I get home. We can both relate because being an entrepreneur is lonely. If something breaks, YOU have to deal with it. But up here it's a community. If the toilet is clogged, they share that responsibility eight ways.

"Do guys ever quit?" I asked. "Just say enough is enough."

"One brother left and married a girl in town. And others have left too, but it's rare," he said. "To become a monk the process can take two to three years. First you're a seeker and then you have a six- to twelve-month candidacy when you live at the monastery. And then psychological evaluations and references are done. Then the candidates ask to come in as a novice; if they're received, they get a new name and then monastic profession... full step of commitment to the vows."

"So, what about the hair?"

"Cutting the hair goes back to Roman days. If you were in someone's service, you would shave your head. That way if you ran away they looked for the bald guy. Now it's a token of rendering service to monastic life."

That made sense. We kept heading up the hill.

"Why aren't any of the drawings on wall in the church of blacks?"

"There is," Stavros said. "Moses the black from Skete, Egyptian. And there's a trend to not represent people totally accurately but to use depictions. That's why most have the same olive skin."

At this point Lenny the Intern was a mile ahead of us. Since Lenny couldn't hear, I realized there was no way to call for him. Brother Mark, Brother Thomas, and I got to the top of the mountain (hill) first and looked everywhere. We waited for Bo and Brother Stavros. And a few minutes later they made it up. The road flattened out at the top of the hill, and it looked like a perfect place for local high school kids to drink a few stolen six packs of beer,

"Where's Lenny? This is against protocol," Bo said. "No hiker can hike alone out here. It's not safe."

He pulled out a whistle from his jacket, blew it, and then started yelling, "LEEE-NNNNY."

"Bo, Lenny is deaf." I said.

I told the group I'd go on a one-man search-and-recovery mission to find Lenny. I went off the road and about a mile down the steep snowy mountain. And then I finally saw Lenny about a quarter mile ahead. I double-stepped my way and caught him in about five minutes.

"Yo," I said. "We gotta stick together."

Lenny just looked at me, so I used my finger to point up. Let's go.

Once we were all back together, we had a quick lunch. It was really nice to be out and away from the monastery. After we finished, we headed back down. There was a lot less talking on the way down, but it was comfortable. We all just enjoyed the nature. When we got to the bottom, I offered to ride home with Bo. I liked my chances of survival better with him. But, on top of being old and cautious, Bo drove like he was in England—on the wrong side of the road.

It might have been safer in Stavros's car.

We stopped at Rite-Aid for Lenny's ear medicine. And I have to say I never realized how much fun a Rite-Aid could be. I felt like Charlie in Willy Wonka's Chocolate Factory. This was the first civilization I've seen in months. Okay, days, but it felt like months. There were real humans at Rite-Aid, and they were walking around like they had lives to lead. There were newspapers, candy, good soaps, products... I didn't know what to do with myself. It was all so glorious.

"They have aspirin," I said to no one. "And Band-Aids!"

I saw an older woman look over at me. I think she thought I was mental because she kept a safe distance between us. I didn't care. I grabbed the Method foam soap pump and said to her: "I love this soap!"

That's when she ducked into another aisle. I didn't want to leave. I bought a newspaper and chocolate. Seriously, it was like being at Disney World for the first time. And I didn't care how long the lines were. I could have stayed there for hours.

I guess this is a great example of how much we take for granted. I mean seriously, I never thought I'd be grateful for a Rite-Aid. Normally I try to avoid going there. It's like some of these chain pharmacy stores actually train their employees to go slowly and make customers wait. Today though—I LOVED IT. I want to go back.

On the drive home to the monastery I held on to my plastic bag like a nine-year-old holding on to his bag of Halloween candy. It was mine. It was all mine. I wasn't going to let go. I was grateful for soap. But why don't I feel like that every time I leave a pharmacy?

8:00 p.m.

So, the diagnosis is back, and Lenny can hear! The ear drops didn't work, so the monks took Lenny to a clinic. Brother Stavros told me they drained about a gallon of wax out of each of Lenny's ears. How can you let a gallon of wax accumulate in your ears? Didn't he ever hear of a Q-tip? A washcloth? After he got back I saw him in the reading room and had my first real conversation.

"Where'd you go to school, Lenny?"

"UNLV."

"Cool. What'd you study?"

"Books."

"Um, do you like this place versus the Indian reservation?"

"Hard to say."

"Okay. Well, what do you have planned next?"

"Undetermined."

"Are you staying here long?"

"Undetermined."

Lenny's lips didn't move when he spoke. Maybe he studied ventriloquism?

"Are you happy up here?"

"Is that a trick question? Joy is fleeting," he said. "Or should I say...happiness is fleeting."

"Huh?"

Silence...

It wasn't going well.

Hiking with Brother Marc, Brother Thomas,
Lenny the Intern, and one of my favorite dogs!

"Maybe I should ask it like this," I said. "What are you looking for, Lenny?" For the first time he stopped looking at my head
and stared at me with his dark eyes. He didn't say a word. "Religion? Direction?" I asked, trying to help him along. "Or are you
not sure and you'll just know when you know?"

"I'm looking for all of the above."

And then he went back to his computer and pretended I
wasn't there.

I think I liked Lenny better when he couldn't hear.

Or do I have some deep-seated desire for Lenny to like me?

That's an underlining theme in my life: I want to be liked. Is
that insecurity or an asset?

Homesick, but getting cheered up by Khan.

DAY 9

Broken or Breakthrough

"Breakthroughs happen when limiting thoughts and behaviors are challenged."

—FABIENNE FREDRICKSON

I woke up feeling sluggish. It wasn't unrest, it was more like restlessness. Perhaps it's the expectations I had coming in. ***Expectations are tricky and often set us up for disappointment.*** I wasn't motivated to go see the sun rise. I don't know why. And as I lay in bed staring at the ceiling I kept thinking about Sara. She'd said something before I left that seemed rather profound, but now I wasn't so sure.

Two nights before I left for the monastery I was out to dinner with Sara and we were chatting about the different things I might be doing here. There was a lot of excitement and anticipation of the unknown. Neither of us had a clue about what living with monks would look like.

And then I asked Sara how long I should stay.

"Stay until you have a breakthrough or you're broken," she said.

It sounded like great advice. And I consider her an expert on this topic. She told me the first time she remembers being on the edge of a breakthrough or being broken. It was when she was fifteen years old and saw her friend get struck by a car and killed. Her friend was riding her bike on a bridge in Florida when it played out before her very eyes. It obviously was a traumatic experience for her. And at the time she had no idea a break-through was even possible.

Around the same time, her parents were getting a divorce. She says that nearly broke her for good. But when her dad was leaving the house for the last time, he handed her a series of Wayne Dyer motivational cassettes. And this was her break-through. Sara started listening to the tapes every day. It helped her deal with the tragedy of her friend and the difficulty of her parents splitting up.

Sara listened to the self-help tapes constantly, over and over again; she couldn't get enough. She listened to them so much that her friends in high school started refusing to get into her car because they couldn't take listening to them anymore. She credits Wayne Dyer CDs and the inner work she did as a big part of her success. ***The gap between breakthroughs and being broken is so narrow that sometimes it's impossible to see.***

What I'm dealing with now is NOTHING close to what Sara went through. But it's a different kind of mindfuck. Sara was dealing with real shit. When I put it in that kind of perspective, it makes it easier. That is until I wait five minutes and get all up in my head again. ***Perspective is such a beautiful thing, but the key is to never let it go when you're holding onto it.*** My grip on perspective isn't as tight as it should be.

I'm not sure if I'm closer to a breakthrough or being broken. It feels like neither.

This afternoon I walked four miles up and down the road. I've been able to stay consistent in getting in around ten miles a day.

Usually I do three miles between breakfast and chores and do the rest in the afternoon after "dinner." While my phone doesn't get a signal, it still has a function that accurately counts my mileage, so I've been bringing it on my walks.

I stayed to the far right of the road because some of the snow melted last night, making the path rather muddy. And I was just walking like normal when I heard a "ding" on my phone. And I felt a vibration. When I looked at it I noticed two texts had found their way onto my phone. And I had one bar of service. ONE BAR...

I moved from the spot I was standing and the bar went away. Wow...

There's one spot on this isolated 500-acre property that gets cell service? And I just found it.

I immediately went back to it and the one bar reappeared.

I started typing a text to my wife.

ME: I love you. I miss you. I miss the kids. Don't forget the kids have soccer today.

As soon as I hit send I saw the little three bubbles forming indicating that Sara was texting me back. I was SO EXCITED. I literally felt like the Professor just fixed the transistor radio on *Gilligan's Island*. I couldn't wait for her to text back...

SARA: Sweetie, today is Tuesday. Not Sunday. Are you okay?
ME: No. It's Sunday. Are you okay?
SARA: Um...I'm okay, but I'm looking at a calendar. Are you sure you're okay?

Really? It's Tuesday?! I started counting on my fingers, and she was right. I'm in the land that time forgot. Time exists only on clocks and calendars. It has no worth at the monastery.

ME: How was soccer on Sunday?

SARA: Funny you should ask. I actually thought it was Saturday on Sunday.

ME: Ha. So no soccer?

SARA: Sorry, no soccer. What have you been doing?

ME: Washing dishes, scrubbing floors, and training dogs.

SARA: What? How are you holding up?

ME: The monks have been great. Nuns too. Also I met a spiritual intern who I thought was trying to kill me. But it turned out he had a gallon of wax in his ears.

SARA: Nuns?

ME: Cool nuns.

SARA: Are there any other kind? Tell me, did you bring enough clothing?

ME: Too much. I have worn the same thing every day.

SARA: What? I'm not surprised.

ME: I haven't even showered yet. How are the kids?

SARA: They miss you a ton, but they're all doing well. Question, do you want to come to LA this weekend with Lazer and me? I'm taking him to Disney. I think it's enough already up there, love.

ME: Disney? That is unbelievable. Of course I want to go, but I don't know.

SARA: We miss you. But we want you to do what's in your heart.

ME: Let me see what I can do. Maybe I'll just come
home tomorrow.

SARA: Okay honey. Just let us know.

ME: Love you.

SARA: Love you too...

And then I saw the bubble on my screen. She was still
typing.

SARA: If you are coming home please take a shower ;)

So today is TUESDAY...I'm not any closer to a breakthrough,
but it felt good to text with Sara. She put a smile on my face. I have
friends who travel all of the time who tell me it makes their marriage
stronger—it's because they spend time away from each other and
really appreciate the time they do have. That makes sense to me,
but right now I really wish I was home. I've missed them enough.

So, I took Sara's advice and took my first shower! I hadn't
really felt the need until now because you just get re-dirty the
next day. But the dirt was sticking to me. I was gross. The
shower was super small, and the showerhead in my bathroom
was installed for someone the size of an eight-year-old. I felt like
one of those yoga masters who can fit inside of a suitcase. There
was an old plastic chair in the shower, so I sat on it to get low
enough to let the water fall on me. Man, did it feel good! But I
still can't kick it. I'm homesick. I miss my wife. My kids.

I'm ready to leave. But is that the bully talking or the truth?

I'm going home tomorrow.

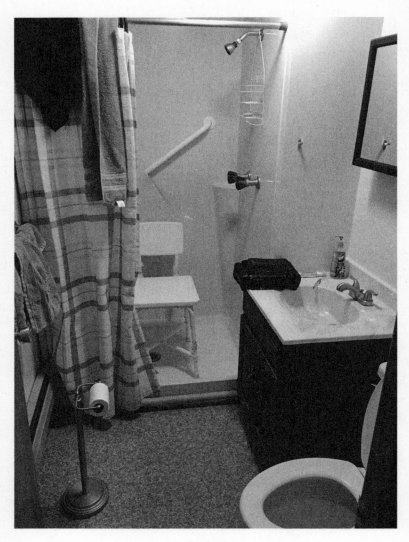

My bathroom.

DAY 10
Honest Moments

"The first big pitfall is to let society define what happiness is."
—BROTHER STAVROS

I got up at 6:00 a.m. It was my last day, so I wanted to do it right. And I've been making a habit of getting up early and stepping outside. My breath made giant puffs in the frigid air, but the cold didn't bother me. There's nothing quite like watching the rising sun. I stood there, taking it all in, knowing I'd be waking up in my own bed tomorrow. I stayed there a little longer than usual. It was as if I was hoping the sun would have an encore. But deep down I knew the credits had already begun to roll.

I briefly looked for Brother Christopher when I got back. I wanted to ask him to call me a car service. But I didn't look too hard because I also wanted to go for one last walk. It was starting to warm up a little bit, so I hit the road. As I was heading back up the hill, Brother Gregory whizzed around the curve in his car. He was coming directly toward me—fast. We made eye contact as I jumped to the side. He gave me the thumbs-up. And then he was out of sight.

I stood there in the snowbank.

Thinking...

Feeling...

Knowing...

And then it hit me...

REMEMBER TOMORROW...

The voice inside my head was screaming louder than Lenny. It just kept saying the same thing over and over: REMEMBER TOMORROW, REMEMBER TOMORROW, REMEMBER TOMORROW. It's one of the mantras I live by. It's the way I beat up the bully in my head. And in that moment I knew I had to remember how tomorrow was going to feel if I pulled the rip cord too soon and went home. Instantly everything changed.

When you come to a point when you have to make a key decision, remember how that choice will make you feel tomorrow, and the tomorrow after that, and the one after that. You want to drop out of the marathon at mile 18? Okay, that's fine, but...remember what it's going to feel like tomorrow when you're left alone to think about it. You want to get drunk and dance on the table at your holiday party? Cool, but...remember how it's going to feel tomorrow when you walk into the office.

And right there on the side of the road I was saying to myself, remember what you're going to feel like tomorrow if you quit too soon. When I climbed Mount Washington with my friends there were times during the hike we all wanted to turn around and call it a day. We were tired, cold, and hungry. As we continued to climb my friend Nick would say, "It's not an honest hike yet. We have to keep going."

What he meant was we still had more work to do. We had to be honest with ourselves about our effort. Yes, we were on the mountain, but we had not exhausted every ounce in our souls. Only by going past the point when we truly thought we had to stop would it be an honest hike. Complete or incomplete, it has to be honest.

I still had more effort to give at the monastery; it wasn't an "honest" trip yet.

Immediately I felt rejuvenated, knowing I was staying longer to push myself. Making that commitment to myself where there was no turning back felt empowering and gave me a second wind. I was all in.

On my walk back to my room I came up with this: You can read *The 7 Habits of Highly Effective People* and listen to 115 Vince Lombardi quotes. You can study *Awaken the Giant Within* and go to ten Tony Robbins lectures. However, the only way to truly get better is to close the book, turn off the Internet, and go out into the world. And stick it out.

When you want to quit...get uncomfortable. And Remember Tomorrow.

We spend so much of our lives trying to avoid pain. We're all wired to seek comfort and I love being comfortable. However, **the real growth comes when you step outside of that comfort zone and tap into your reserve tank.** That's where you see what you're made of, and that's often the place you feel most alive. And that's the other beauty of REMEMBER TOMORROW— when you truly lay it all out there today, tomorrow is even better.

Now, the truth is, learning by doing can be a lot harder than learning online or from a book. When you immerse yourself in something, like I did with SEAL and now the monks, there can be times when you want to just pack up and go home. It takes mental toughness and fortitude to complete a new experience. But the experience also needs to be HONEST. And that's on you. I'm the only person who can say if my stay at the monastery is honest or not.

And I know in my heart that it's not, not yet, but it will be...

I've heard that grit is the best indicator of future success. Well, this is becoming the ultimate test of my resilience. It's not like other challenges I've done in my life. Strangely I like pain, cramps, and a little blood trickling down my shin. It reminds me I'm alive. And, sure, a photo of me looking busted up, sweating, and on the verge of a collapse competing in an endurance event looks pretty gritty hanging on my wall. But I truly like that feeling.

I'll tell you what I don't like: being away from my family, slowing down, left alone to think and reflect all day, doing chores, and not having the comforts of my regular life. So for me to stay here takes some grit. The easy thing would be to go home; to tell myself I stuck it out for a couple of days and pack my bags. But that's what my internal enemy has been singing the last ten days, and he's got a whole choir backing him up.

I signed up for fifteen days, and that's what I need to do.

If I didn't I wouldn't be exercising my mental toughness muscle. That'd be like saying it's okay to not finish what I started. One time I asked SEAL if he ever quit something because he was tired. I don't quit when I'm tired, he said. I quit when I'm done.

Regret can hurt just as much as physical pain and sometimes last longer. If I had cut my monastery stay short, I know I'd have regretted it long after I left. It's easy to get caught up in the real-time moment and emotions, but that's short-term thinking. When you fast-forward and project the future feelings of your decision, you often get clarity and can fight the "quit demon."

A few years ago I was doing a thirty-mile stand-up paddle board race around Manhattan. The competition started at Chelsea Piers, headed up past Columbia University, and then crossed over to the East River before ending down by Brooklyn. The currents were incredibly unpredictable and brutally challenging. At times you could paddle as hard as humanly possible and not move twelve yards. And when you stopped to rest you'd get pushed forty feet in the opposite direction.

When I showed up I knew I was in trouble. The competitors looked like Jeff Spicoli on steroids—Hawaiian surfer dudes with super aquatic endurance. They had hydration systems attached to their deck pads. Goos and Power Bars were duct-taped to their boards, and intricate navigation devices were installed on their aerodynamic stand-ups. I had nothing except for the board I purchased online ONE WEEK before the race; it was around the same time I got the idea to enter.

When I got to the starting area, I immediately noticed my paddleboard was way shorter than all the other boards, way heavier, and *definitely* not aerodynamic. *Shit...*

To make my board lighter I decided to put all of my supplies (water, food, sunscreen, AND lifejacket) in a canoe my friends Mike and Rob Young rented. I figured I'd be better off having them haul it than carrying it myself in a knapsack for ten hours.

"Just stay close to me," I told them. "You'll be my crew team."

As soon as the race started, 100 paddlers took off and spread across the Hudson in a frenzy. I was headed thirty miles directly into the wind. The currents were super strong. It was hot—like 101 degrees hot. And my board was built for someone shorter than I am and for cruising around a recreational lake. I was fucked.

About a quarter mile into the rough sea I turned around, and the Young brothers, my crew team, were nowhere to be seen. I knew at that moment I had to get through the whole race on my own. I wanted to quit. I didn't though because of my motto: Remember Tomorrow. If I quit, I knew I was going to hate the feeling the next day and even probably a month from then. I had to gut out thirty miles with no water, food, or sunscreen. I broke the race into many smaller pieces and goals and began to chip away. Just keep chipping away, I repeated to myself. Nine hours later, I finished!

Are there times when quitting is the right thing to do? Of course, but **quitting just because it's easier is never the right decision. It only takes a minute to quit, but the moment will replay in your mind tomorrow, and the tomorrow after that, and the one after that**.

Mental toughness is an art form, but like any art form it takes practice. It's a muscle that has to be exercised consistently. Meditating, praying, quieting the mind, manual labor, and being present are difficult for me, but I know challenging myself is going to pay big dividends. If I quit today, I'll feel lousy about myself tomorrow.

The rest of the day felt different—better.

I spent a lot of time with Brother Mark. The plan has been for me to rotate my morning chores with a different brother. That way I can get to know each of the monks more intimately and learn what each one does to keep the monastery afloat. I've already worked with Thomas in the dog training center and tending to the dogs at night, with Stavros cleaning the church, with Brother Mark cleaning the dishes and Brother Gregory preparing the guest house, and I'll be with Brother Ambrose smoking cheese in the next day or so. I'll also be spending time with other monks at the grooming and breeding center.

Brother Mark is really friendly. It's like hanging out with an old friend. He leads the prayer services and is in charge of the kitchen. While Josh the Cook comes in to prepare several meals, Brother Mark often cooks and cleans on behalf of all as well. Brother Mark looks like he's a forty-year-old tennis pro at a fancy country club, with piercing blue eyes, a fit build, and an amazingly friendly disposition. As it turns out, Brother Mark is a health nut, so we hit it off right away. He was fascinated by the fact that I have only eaten fruit until noon for the last twenty-seven years.

"Isn't that too much sugar?" he asked.

I explained that the sugar in fruit is one of the most misunderstood concepts as it relates to diet. We spent hours talking about the principles of Harvey Diamond's book *Fit for Life*. Fruit is the perfect food if eaten correctly. That means on an empty stomach and eating it with no other food.

"The less energy you use on digestion, the more energy you have for everything else," I explained.

"I'll have to try it," he said.

After my time with Brother Mark, Brother Stavros told me to follow him to the library. The monks have accumulated thousands of books over the last fifty years and have integrated a sophisticated system of logging and managing all the books. In fact, they use the same system that the Library of Congress does to manage their inventory. As we walked through the rows of books it was fascinating to see the categories and the collection they had amassed. Religious books, business books, diet books, travel books...you name it, they had it.

It was a great day. Ironic that my breakthrough came via something I've known all along...my effort has to be honest.

Now it feels like I've gotten a second wind, but I'm not going to sprint to the finish; that's not very monkish. I'm going to stay focused on being present, think about my breathing, and stride to wherever the finish line might be.

And do you want to know how intuitive the monks are? I was sitting at breakfast this morning, and we were talking about the decision process to become a monk. One brother turned to me and said, *"It's really very simple. Decide that you want it more than you're afraid of it."*

DAY 11
Lunch with the Nuns

"God has not called me to be successful; He has called me to be faithful."

—MOTHER TERESA

I watched the sun rise. But this time it was as if someone turned on a snow machine. It was coming down from all directions. I retreated to my cell because I wanted to get ready for my big day. I was invited to have lunch with the nuns—something I never thought I'd ever say. I shook and kicked off the snow as I entered my room.

I wanted to jot some stuff down, so I started looking through my backpack for a pen. I lost mine overnight somehow. As I rummaged through my bag I found a piece of paper. I forgot I brought it. Written on it was a morning passage from the Dalai Lama I copied down before I left. My plan was to recite it the first thing every morning:

"Every day, think as you wake up, 'Today I am fortunate to have woken up, I am alive. I have a precious human life, I am not going to waste it. I am going to use all my energies to develop myself, to expand my heart out to others, to achieve enlightenment for the benefit of all beings. I am going to have kind thoughts

towards others, I am not going to get angry or think badly about others. I am going to benefit others as much as I can.'"

At breakfast Stavros offered to drive me to the nuns' house because of the storm. Due to his driving I wanted to say, "It's okay, I'm going to walk," but when I looked out of my window I decided to roll the dice and take the ride. It was snowing really hard. He told me he'd meet me in my room about ten minutes before I was supposed to arrive for my lunch. When he walked in he was wearing a heavy winter coat that looked like he got it from Sir Edmund Hillary. It must have weighted 200 pounds. I was wearing a light ski jacket. When he saw me he asked if my coat was a "moon jacket." He was mesmerized by the technology of it. He couldn't believe that man was able to make a jacket so lightweight and keep you so warm.

"Is that special ordered from NASA?"

"No, Stavros, I actually just got it from REI."

"What's REI?"

"Oh, I'm sorry, that's a store that sells outdoor clothing and gear."

"And that little parka you're wearing can keep you warm?"

"Yes, it's a down coat."

"It's amazing . . . just amazing . . . all these advances."

I thought to myself, I can take a picture on my phone and text it to someone in China and they'll get the exact image in 0.01 seconds . . . and he's marveling about a lightweight jacket that keeps me warm. These guys are really behind the curve.

The snowstorm smacked me in the face as we walked up to the parking lot. He unlocked a car door, and I quickly jumped into an old Subaru. This wasn't the car we drove to the hike, but it had the same vibe. It's just a car, very basic, like a floor and a motor—that's it. I don't think they opted for any of the upgrades at the dealership. NONE! It's kind of like riding in a bumper car.

Brother Stavros told me to lock the door—manually.

The front seat was adjusted for a monk who's five feet four, so the bucket was as close to the windshield as the manufacturer allowed. Either that or one of the monks illegally slid it more toward the dashboard to give a Dwight Howard–sized guest leg-room in the back. Like six feet eleven inches legroom. I doubt the Charlotte Hornet's center was a guest, here so I assume it's just positioned that way for now. Whatever the case, my forehead was touching the windshield.

But the monks have been preaching gratitude, and I was grateful for the ride.

My knees were in my chest, forcing my balls into my stom-ach. It wasn't pleasant. I reached back with my right hand and tried to recline back to give myself some relief. And as luck would have it Stavros chimed in, "Oh, the recliner lever has been jammed for several years."

In that moment it hit me. There's a children's book here somewhere—*The Coat and the Car*. Stavros was fascinated by my coat and the modern-day technology of it. And I was fascinated by the simplicity of his car. It made me wonder: Are these guys missing out being so far behind the times, or are they actually keeping ahead, from an intellectual standpoint, by not keeping up? I bet if I lived up here I'd learn something new from Stavros every day.

I stayed jammed against the windshield for the entire ride to the nuns' house. I wanted to be on my best behavior because having lunch with nuns is scary. Nuns aren't scary, but the possibilities of offending a nun seem limitless. Sara once tried to get me to go to etiquette school because of my table manners. I don't think I'm rude or uncouth, but I just see eating as the same thing as the gas station—fill it up—unleaded. As we approached the nuns' house I wished I'd taken the etiquette course.

I wasn't worried I was going to mess up the lunch; we'll call it aware of the potential dangers and comfortably cautious. My views on mealtime have already shifted in my short stay. I've noticed how special it is at the monastery. We eat at the exact time every day. This involves sacrifice because the meal and the time together takes precedence over everything else—there are no excuses to not show up. It never gets pushed back. Mealtime is set in stone, and attendance is mandatory. And all of that is important. It's been said that family dinner is one of the best things you can do for a lasting marriage.

I made a mental note to incorporate more family meals when I get back. And some prayer; when the monks say grace it's a form of gratitude. That small "thanks" every day is powerful. I want to implement it at home. When I was in my twenties I wrote ten handwritten letters every day to thank people. And then I mailed them. So many wonderful things have grown from those letters, but most importantly I could feel gratitude. It flowed daily.

And inversely, the time we have at the monastery before the meal is more productive because of it. We know what has to get done by a certain time. So I'm learning to appreciate mealtime much more and trying to get as much out of it as I can. But as important as mealtime is for the monks, you'd think it gets a little boring after fifty years with the same people—but not for them. It's a moment of the day to come together, be present, and enjoy.

I got dropped off in front of the nuns' house. It felt like I was in middle school and my dad just drove me to the movie theater. I waved goodbye as Brother Stavros peeled out of the driveway and fishtailed onto the snow-covered road.

I turned around and looked at the house. It was built in 1971 by the nuns. I was told they took a woodshop class in town to learn how to use a band saw and frame a house, etc. I've read that **the number one thing to accomplishing a goal is choosing a goal that you deeply desire**. I had amazing respect for the nuns for taking the initiative and accomplishing their goal. The house oozed of passion.

Sister Cecilia greeted me with her dog. I put my hand down low with my knuckles facing the dog's mouth just as I was taught. The dog sniffed my hand and then my ass. Apparently he or she approved because the dog laid down for a belly scratch. I obliged.

Sister Cecilia gave me a tour of the house and bakery. It felt like a very nice bed and breakfast—warm and inviting. There was carpet, and it was super clean. Attached to the house was a fully equipped and operating bakery that looked like it belonged in ANYTOWN, U.S.A.

When I asked where she was from, she said, "I'm a Hoosier."

Sister Cecilia is one cool nun.

Two young women from the divinity school at Yale joined us. They're staying with the sisters for a few days, and I saw them at the service this morning. One said she was from Oregon. "Oh, you're a Duck?"

Sister Cecilia paused and looked over at me like I'd sinned.

I guess she only knows the Big Ten.

Before we got started the two young women stood across from me in the dining room as we waited. I guess they're nuns-in-training, or prospective nuns—I wasn't sure what to call them. But one of them seemed really angry; the other was sweet and angelic. I think the nice one was named Debbie. Since we were alone I tried to make small talk. I figured they had to be friendlier than Lenny.

But I wanted to be careful. I haven't seen my wife in over a week and have been sequestered with a bunch of forty- to seventy-year-old men around the clock. I felt like these two gals haven't been around any men either, so I wanted to be clear about my intention or maybe I should say lack of intention.

"Hey, I'm Jesse. I'm married," I said, grabbing a glass of water off the table. "And have four kids. How are we all doing today? Good?"

"Hi, married Jesse," the friendly nun-in-training said.

"What are you doing here anyway?" the angry nun-in-training chimed in.

"I'm what you call a guest. Just visiting."

Debbie started asking questions in a rapid-fire machine gun way. It was like she took the vow of silence and I was the first human she could talk to. I couldn't keep up.

Have you found God? And I'm also curious, what authors inspire you? You can learn a lot about people that way. Have you surrendered your life to the Lord at a micro level? How long have you been here, and what have you learned?

"I've learned a lot," I said, trying to catch up. "I learn every day."

"Like what?"

I felt like I was onstage at the Miss America Pageant. Like this was my final question to see if I had a chance at winning the crown. The way these young women were looking at me made me feel like I was being judged. I needed this to be good.

"The irony in the word 'present.'"

They both looked confused. I needed to avoid a Miss South Carolina response...

"If you're present in doing a task it's like receiving a present. There's joy in everything we do. And being present is an integral part of it. Sometimes it can be difficult. Our minds like to wander. But if I just say out loud what I'm doing I can always bring myself back to center—to be present. Like the other day I was washing dishes and my mind was all over the place. I just said, "I'm washing dishes," and instantly I was right back to where I needed to be—washing dishes."

"I'm not sure I'm following. Can you explain?"

"We all have had moments where we are HERE but not present. We miss a basket at our son's basketball game because we were checking Facebook. We live in a world where we can watch real-time events unfold all over the world live, yet we can't focus on where we are right now."

"I get that. What else have you learned?" the nice one asked.

"That **there's no lid to happiness. I can always improve.**"

"Can you feel religion? And God all day?"

"Well, actually," I said. "There are really only two things going on up here, prayer and labor. Religion and spirituality are a big part of it, but prayer is only in the morning and night. In between the two services is labor. So you only get the religious element twice a day. But that's only technically speaking because it does surround us."

"When the monks work do they feel like God is steering them?"

"I don't know," I said. "Ask them. But I don't think so. I think they're just working."

"But they're doing God's work."

"No," I said. "They're selling puppies to keep the lights on. I'm kidding...well, sort of. I think they're in constant contact with God. And searching for God's will. But the one thing I've noticed is they have extreme passion for every task they do. Everything. I assume that's because it's their place. They're cutting their own grass. The other thing is nobody says no to the commitment to the community. Everyone is at dinner. Everyone is at the meeting. Everyone is at prayer."

"Is this experience everything you thought it would be?"

"Interestingly enough, no," I said. "Most of the spiritual traditions I assumed about the monastery aren't true—not even close. My expectations were way off the mark. It hasn't been a series of mountaintop experiences where I felt free to explore my spirituality unobstructed by the hitches of daily life. It's a grind up here too—everyone is expected to contribute in a series of tedious duties. But there's regularity to it, and the monks hold that regularity sacred. There's really not much room for deviation. But it's been a great catalyst for personal transformation for me. *I've learned that spiritual time doesn't have to be carved out; I can explore the spiritual life when I'm doing mundane, trivial work.* The spiritual GoPro is always on the Record setting. My greatest realization up here came when I was scrubbing the church floor."

"What was it?"

"Every task is important. Every moment has purpose."

"Well then, what are you looking for?"

"I'm not really looking as much as I'm experiencing. And we'll see what I get. I'm picking up valuable tips along the way. For example, the brothers know they have to live with each other, so they want to live in peace. How great is that? They have allotted time every week to communicate with each other and sort out any issues. It sounds simple, but an effort needs to be made. I'm going to institute that with my wife when I get home. It'll just mean more peace. Isn't that great?"

"I don't want peace," the angry one finally chimes in.

"Well, the opposite of peace is turmoil," I said. "You want turmoil?"

"NO, I WANT TRUTH," she said, pounding her fist on the table.

Debbie giggled. She seemed really sweet.

"How about you?" I asked. "What are you looking for?"

"I've been trying to find a purpose," Debbie said. "I'm looking for a sign. But I don't know because I keep waiting. I'm super focused on looking for it, but I haven't found it yet."

"Maybe by looking for one thing you miss out on everything else." I said. "I've realized that just experiencing, instead of having expectations and searching, can sometimes be better."

Just then the three real nuns walked into the room.

We all sat for lunch. I looked around the room, and the realization I was eating lunch with three nuns, two nuns-in-training, and three German shepherds hit me. The only interaction I'd ever had with a nun is watching Sally What's-Her-Name in *The Flying Nun*, a television show I watched as a kid staying home from school when I was sick or fake sick—same thing.

On the menu today was fish, which I don't eat, salad, polenta, and cauliflower. The polenta and vegetables were good. One of the sisters had heard I'd partnered with Warren Buffett in the jet business. So she told me she wasn't a fan of his. But I'm pretty sure she was talking about Jimmy Buffett. It's just a hunch.

And then Sister Rebecca told me about a friend of hers who said she only had "three years of work left" and then she was going to "retire and do what she really wants to do" for the rest of her life. Sister Rebecca felt bad for her because she already was doing exactly what she wanted every day of her life.

"Imagine all the time my friend lost not doing what she wanted to do."

I agreed.

So I told her a story about a friend of mine. He's turning fifty-three and is going through something of a change in his life. Getting older can be a rude awakening. All of sudden, the years have gone by and you haven't done nearly what you hoped to do. And the older you get the faster the clock ticks. My friend was in one of those melancholy, what-have-I-done-with-my-life moods. So I said to him, what if I gave you $10 million, what would you do?

"That's easy. I'd move to California first thing," he said.

"Well, guess what? Nobody is going to give you $10 million. But if you want to move to California, do it now."

"Really?"

"Yes. Save up six months of cushion, move, and figure it out. Otherwise you'll live with massive regret."

"Did he move to California?" Debbie asked.

"Nah, he's still talking about it."

People are always waiting for something to happen before they change their lives. But they have it backward; when you change your life, big things are more likely to

happen. One thing is for sure, if you keep waiting for someone to give you $10 million, nothing is going to change.

The nuns and monks have it right. They made the big change in their lives years ago. And you know what would happen if someone gave them $10 million? Nothing...they wouldn't do a damn thing differently. And they'd stay perfectly happy. The takeaway is that money isn't the life changer. Quicksilver cash might upgrade the things in your life, but it does little to alter the course of it. Change costs no money at all. The younger you make decisions to live life on your terms and do what you love to do, the more fulfilling a life you'll live. And it's never too late.

After the main course, lunch got weird. Debbie, the nice nun-in-training, announced she was confused. She grew up in the Georgia Bible Belt and had been told to dress modestly and to wait until she was married to have sex. But she's been hooking up with guys and wasn't sure how to balance it all. And then she asked, "How do you women deal without sex?"

That's when I offered to leave and Sister Cecilia agreed it was probably a good time to go.

Before I left, I surprised them with a gift of Atlanta Hawks T-shirts.

Sister Patricia held hers up and asked for a medium.

And then she asked who Millsap was; she thought it was an unusual name.

I explained it was his last name and his first name is Paul.

"We wear our last names on the jerseys."

"Isn't that self-centered? If it's a team why not only wear the team name and de-emphasize the individual?"

That made sense to me.

With the amazing nuns of New Skete.

"Anyway, Paul," she said. "He sounds religious."

"I'll have to check on that one."

When I got back to the monastery a great surprise was waiting for me. Under my door was a *New York Post*. Josh the Cook snuck it in for me. He's hopefully going to do it every day. We sort of made a side deal. The deal was he'd try to get me a paper and I wouldn't die of boredom. Look, I'm over the hump of wanting to quit, but it's still not easy to be completely isolated. And I was looking forward to reading it.

But Trump was pissed at someone. A white supremacist killed an African American on Ninth Avenue. Terrorists killed four people in Europe. I threw it out before I even got to Page Six's gossip. The day-to-day madness is not something I'm missing. In fact, I'm beginning to enjoy being away from it.

DAY 12
Fitting In

"To find happiness you must be exposed to things.
Happiness is out there...it's your job to look."

—THE MONKS OF NEW SKETE

When I walked to the church this morning Lenny the Intern sprinted past me. He stopped underneath the tower and begged Luke to let him ring the bells. Luke obliged. Lenny put on the huge protective headphones and started to wail on the bells. I slipped into the empty church and sat at my usual spot. The bells sounded louder than normal. I give Lenny credit; he played them like he was in Iron Maiden.

"WAY TO GO, LENNY," I said when he entered.

And I got my first smile. He looked truly happy. After service, the two of us headed to breakfast. We didn't talk, but just walking together is a dramatic improvement in our relationship.

When we entered into the dining room, Raisa and Verna, the German shepherds, stood at attention. They do this every time they see Lenny. I didn't get it. Not before today. Lenny is maybe the most antisocial person I know, but the dogs love him. I'm one of the most social people I know, and the dogs pay me no mind. I was starting to think Lenny was some kind of secret dog whisperer. The Keyword being "was."

We were allowed to talk at breakfast, so I asked the monks if they could have dinner with three people who were alive, who would they choose? They immediately threw it back to me, but I was prepared. I told them how I was recently at a dinner party with ten couples and was asked that very question. Most of the others at the party had already said the obvious choices: "Gates, Oprah, Buffett, Obama, Musk, etc.," but when it was my turn my three choices were rappers. A few heads were scratched because they couldn't understand. But the reason I chose them was because these guys had an impact on me when I was fourteen years old. And they changed the trajectory of my life. So I wanted to meet them and thank them. I wanted to ask how they mastered their craft and what their creative process was like. My angle was coming more from personal impact.

That night driving home with Sara I thought about it: Why not actually do it? So the next day I invited ten of the most influential artists in my life to my house for dinner...and six weeks later they were all seated around my dinner table. My friends all asked me how I got them to come and I said simply, "I asked."

Nothing happens without asking for it.

Dinner was amazing. The similarities in their journey as musicians to mine as an entrepreneur were evident. For starters, they were so young when they started, they had no time to be scared. As someone starting out in business, **getting over the fear of being embarrassed is one of the most liberating gifts you can give yourself.** I don't like to be embarrassed (I don't think any of us do), but I'm not afraid of it. The dinner lasted well into the wee hours, and it was an incredible experience for me. I realize most people don't get to do something like that, so I felt incredibly fortunate.

The monks loved the story and started throwing out the names for their wish-list guests. All of the people were religious leaders and philosophers. They were the men and women who helped shape their own personal development during their journey. Then I asked if they had any interest in meeting anyone famous, and Brother Christopher said, "It doesn't matter what others are doing, it matters what you are doing."

Amen.

10:00 a.m.

So today's chore was grooming with Brother Luke and Lenny. After we ate, I did the dishes and headed out. The grooming center is connected to the whelping house where all the puppies are. I pushed open the door as I walked in and hit Lenny in the back. He was standing facing the wall. Just standing there frozen. It was like someone had put him in the corner. He didn't look well, so I immediately asked if he was alright.

"NOOOO. All the barking is messing with my mind. Make it STOP. I'M NOT OK."

I didn't know what to do. He looked like he was ready to snap.

So I told Brother Luke he had better come quick and help Lenny. Luke tugged Lenny by the arm and pulled him into the grooming room. It was like a scene out of soap opera. He grabbed him and shook the crazy out of him, at least for the time being.

Grooming, I learned, is an all-day event. With the three of us and two German shepherds, Shems and Khan, it was like the number 6 train at rush hour—there was nowhere to move.

There's a big wooden table the dogs climb up on, with a brush, nail clipper, sprayer, and everything else we needed within hand's reach. We started with Khan. He jumped on the table.

"Plotz," Brother Luke said to Khan. Khan immediately sat down.

Apparently, the New Skete German shepherds are authentic—they speak perfect German.

The monks keep a satellite radio in the grooming room, and Brother Luke flipped it on. Who knew? The dial was set to NPR. I'm not sure who was live, but it sounded like Terry Gross. And then Luke explained to us that the dogs love this station and they also are into Gregorian chant music. Watching him with the dogs is like watching myself with my children. He's deeply connected and engaged. He loves them and enjoys caring for them so much. And the way the dogs respond to him is amazing. They love him just as much.

Brother Luke doesn't raise dogs—he raises spiritual guides.

But it was time to work, so he did all of the preliminary stuff like clipping and brushing while Lenny and I watched. And then he grabbed the electric filer and started trimming the dog's nails. Lenny and I were basically hugging at this point to give Brother Luke enough room. And since I was two inches from Lenny's face I figured it was time to build on our relationship. I asked Lenny if he's a big fan of dogs.

"Obviously—I grew up with farm animals."

But I thought he came from Vegas? And he was just flipping out a minute ago.

When Luke finished Khan's haircut, it was Shems's turn. Our job was to keep Khan company while Shems got groomed. I wrapped my arms around the shepherd, but Lenny had like one finger on the dog and had moved as far away as he could. That's when Brother Luke started gushing about Lenny of how much the dogs love him.

When we were done, Lenny couldn't wait to get out of there. Again, we went through the whelping room and there was a litter of pups. Brother Luke scooped one of them up and tried to hand it to me. I didn't want to take the puppy. What if I dropped him? What if he peed on me? What if he hated the way I smelled? But before I could say something he was plopped into my hands. I held the little ball of fur close to my chest. The pup nuzzled in for the warmth. Its eyes were still closed.

Their eyes don't open until they're six days old, so the puppy doesn't know who or what is holding it, yet it's completely trusting. At first I felt a little uneasy holding the little fella. I was worried I was doing it wrong. But he melted into my chest, and I began to pet him.

Tonight at supper we had blueberries for dessert. And when we finished we all stood up to pray. Everyone had their heads down and eyes closed. Brother Christopher started to lead us. And as he spoke I couldn't help it; I opened an eye to see if anyone else was looking. That's when I saw Lenny slipping Verna a blueberry underneath the table. And then he fed one to Shems. He's bribing them! When I looked over again, Lenny's eyes were closed. It was like he'd been deep in prayer the whole time. Dog whisperer, my ass.

Later we all gathered in the reading room where they had an extra TV set up. It was movie night. When I first heard about it

I got really excited. I was thinking *Animal House* and popcorn. What a great night! The monks have been raving about it all day too. "Jesse, are you excited for tonight?" and "Only a few hours until the show starts." and "Big night, it's MOVIE NIGHT!"

I headed over there about five minutes early thinking I should try to get a good seat, but most of the monks were already there. I could tell they were genuinely excited to step away from work and prayer and disappear into a good film. I sandwiched myself between Stavros and Thomas on a tiny couch. After a few more minutes, everyone had arrived and it was time to press play.

"I think you're going to like this," Stavros said. "It is part nine, but you shouldn't have any problems following along."

"Oh cool," I said.

Now I was thinking he must mean like the ninth episode of a series, which is fine by me, I'm just excited to escape and get some old-fashioned entertainment. But then Stavros explained we were watching a fourteen-part series about Christianity. Wait, what? That's got to be like a lawyer watching *Law & Order* or a doctor watching *Grey's Anatomy*. Wouldn't they be tired of watching what they do all day?

"We started in November," Stavros added. "We'll be done with the programming by the summer."

Okay, this gives new meaning to binge watching. It's going to take them over six months to finish this series. And once the opening credits rolled I knew why. It was so boring. I couldn't follow the plot, if there was a plot. Regardless, nothing was making sense. I tried. I really tried. I focused on the screen, but it was like watching a foreign film without subtitles. And yet this is the only thing available to watch.

Meanwhile, when I'm at home I get frustrated sometimes with too much content. I spend an hour clicking around Netflix, Hulu, and Amazon but never make a decision. It's like I go window shopping instead of actually consuming entertainment or something educational. I just keep clicking.

But here at the monastery it's like 1977. Growing up we had basically three stations to choose from, and if we wanted to change the channel we actually had to get up off the couch, walk to the television, and manually turn the knob. And if Jimmy Carter or Ronald Reagan was delivering a speech—forget about it—that was an eight-year-old's worst nightmare—three stations—and only one choice. That was frustrating.

As I bounced between 2017 and 1977 in my head, I thought about *Goldilocks and the Three Bears*—strange, right? But in the fairytale Goldilocks tries three chairs, three bowls of porridge, and three beds. And each time she finds her third choice to be "just right."

She keeps trying until she finds something that works for her—just right.

Maybe I should be more like Goldilocks—keep trying things until it's just right.

After about ten minutes of trying to follow the monks' entertainment choice, I looked around the room. And all of the monks were enthralled. They looked like my kids watching *Finding Nemo*. They were hooked. Even Lenny seemed entertained. He was sitting on the edge of his seat like he was watching the final episode of *Homeland*.

I looked over at Raisa and Shems lying on the floor. The two dogs looked back at me like they were asking for help. They were just as bored as I was. I smiled. And then they both slowly got up and walked over to me. They laid next to my feet. Raisa turned her neck and looked up, I rubbed her belly. And then Shems, not wanting to miss out on any of the affection, positioned himself to get the dual belly rub going.

Would Sara kill me if I brought a dog home?

Day 12 is a wrap, but I feel different, like I have a new perspective.

So here I was, fully aware of the contrast that took place. It started with me talking about having ten influential rappers at my house for dinner and then witnessing two of the more mundane activities that occur at the monastery—the grooming of the dogs and the wildly boring viewing of the movie. Could I really be content with the mundane? Could I find enlightenment and value in similar activities once I got back to Atlanta?

DAY 13
35,000 Decisions

"When you talk, you are only repeating what you already know. But if you listen, you may learn something new."

—DALAI LAMA

Monotasking has become second nature. I enjoy washing dishes and cleaning floors. It's amazing how much better my production is when I focus solely on one task. There's no race anymore. I finish when I finish. I finish when the job is done.

That's one thing I'm picking up here at the monastery. **The monks have eliminated most of the self-imposed deadlines that we all put on ourselves daily. Rather, they have shifted their focus to emphasize the quality of their work.** They finish when the job is thoroughly done, and then and only then are they finished. That attitude favors a "no cutting corners style," and the end result is always much better.

Everything around here is improving for me as well. I know when to stand, kneel, and sit during service. I'm starting to learn the prayers and find myself singing along. It feels good to sing in church! When I get home, I want to have the family sing together on Sundays.

The monastery is beginning to feel like my second home. Yesterday, a visitor asked me when the service started, and after

I told them, they said thank you, BROTHER...that's right—Brother Jesse at your service...I'm in the groove. I'm feeling monktastic.

I'm also thinking super clearly, and a new wave of creativity has hit. I think I know why. The average American makes something like 35,000 decisions a day; I read somewhere that we make so many decisions, it can cause a condition called decision fatigue. Ever wonder why late in the game your quarterback decides to throw a pass into triple coverage? Or just before bedtime you decide to let your kid have a candy bar? Or after a hard day's work you think it's a good time to tell your significant other they might have put on a couple of pounds?

Decision fatigue. It hits us all.

But here at the monastery virtually all my decisions have been removed. I eat when the monks tell me to eat. I eat whatever they serve. I don't have to choose from a lot of clothing, I've only worn two outfits. **We don't realize that our daily decisions take up so much space in our heads, there's no room left for creativity and more productive thought.**

With most decisions off my plate now, my brain is flooded with clear thoughts. I went to my room today and organized my entire life into a few short lists. I broke it into four buckets: Family, Work, Personal, and Wellness. And then I filled each category with what I want to accomplish. I saved them on my phone.

I also feel like I'm reconnected to my gut and the force is reentering my body.

My instincts are starting to come alive.

I'm glad I stayed.

I spoke with Sara today on the monks' landline. It was great to hear her voice and get an update on the kids. You know, just the usual four young children carnage and chaos. I feel bad she has to pick up so much slack while I'm gone. I'm going to have to figure out a way to make it up to her. Right after we spoke I meditated again.

Drumroll please... I made it twenty minutes without looking at the clock!

My mind only wandered a few times, and I was able to immediately bring myself back.

I went up to Brother Christopher after service. He'd spent much of his time talking about anxiety and worrying. While listening to him throughout my journey I have realized how tense my body was. And this wasn't just in the moment—it was all the time. My shoulders have always been really tight, and I've tried everything from chiropractors to professional masseuses walking on my back—nothing has ever worked. Today for the first time in years that pain and tightness went away.

"Thank you," I said to Brother Christopher. "Your words really resonated. I don't have so much to worry about in my life. But it seems like I still worry."

"Well, most of us feel overwhelmed. It's usually with things of no real significance," he said.

"What do you mean?"

"We think about things that may happen, everything that can go wrong, and we obsess. Most of the concerns are self-imposed."

I started to go through the checklist of worries on my mind. What if my kids don't do well at school? What if I get sick before the marathon I've been training for? What if my hair doesn't grow back?

"So, is it possible to NOT be anxious?" I asked.

"Well, we all know super inspiring people who live in the midst of tragedy but still live with peace. Pope Francis, who lived in the slums of Argentina, and concentration camp survivors from the Holocaust are great examples. They know suffering deeply but were not robbed of peace."

"Wow. Is there a formula or a blueprint that allows us to be peaceful without turning off our heads?"

"Yes," he said. "Meditating on scripture. Grounding us against whatever threatens us in life. God's words can speak to us and touch us personally if we read a passage multiple times."

I'm not at all religious, but his message still made sense. We kept talking, and I learned that 90 percent of the things we worry about never come to fruition. That isn't a very good return on your investment. Obviously the answer isn't not to worry at all, but we need to keep in check the things out of our control. *If we spend too much time worrying about things that might happen, we'll miss out on all of the things we can improve in our lives.*

I also spent time with Brother Gregory in the monks' gift shop. It was just like two old friends chatting. And then Brother Thomas popped up out of nowhere. I've come to learn that monks might be world-class hide-and-seek players. They're always popping up out of nowhere. I thanked them and told them how it's been an amazing experience for me so far.

"You all have been so welcoming to me, and I really appreciate it. It's been amazing to watch the love that you guys have for each other, the sense of family, and the tremendous work ethic."

"Well, thank you."

"No, thank you. You followed your heart and created the life you wanted to live. And with no focus on money, ego, or competition you have been able to find deep happiness, love, and gratitude. That is a powerful lesson to take home."

"We've gained more than we gave," Brother Gregory said. "We'll miss your energy."

It made me feel good. He gave me some mediation and prayer books and *How to Be Your Dog's Best Friend* and *The Art of Raising a Puppy*, two of the monks' bestselling dog-training books. He put them in a bag and handed them to me with a warm handshake.

A few hours later...

Brother Christopher popped his head into my room. The prayer service wasn't for another two hours, so he asked what I was going to do until then...

"Think," I said.

I'm comfortable being alone.

I sat between Brother Christopher and Brother Stavros for our nightly meal. I'm leaving the monastery tomorrow because I committed to do a podcast in Manhattan. So it was like my last supper. They told me they were impressed I made it this long. I am too. Thirteen days, 120 miles up and down the driveway, fifty hours of religious services, meditating an hour a day the best I can.

Brother Christopher told me that someone had come up to the monastery for a planned stay and only lasted six hours. Well, at least he outlasted Turney. The visitor told the monks the silence got to him and if he stayed there any longer he might freak out. They weren't sure if he unpacked. It makes me think back to my first day. I had no idea what I was getting myself into. I thought there'd be fifty bald monks walking around in robes and sandals in complete silence.

Right before I went to bed I asked Brother Stavros what he missed most about life on the outside. He said the screened-in porch in Georgetown where he grew up. Fifty years and the only thing Stav misses is a porch? Wow. He said he can still smell the grass and flowers like it was yesterday. It makes me wonder what I'll miss in twenty-five years. The difference in how we perceive time is mad. Fifty years in the monastery went by like a shot for him. For me, the two weeks feels like a year.

I recently told Sara that I wanted to throw a big party in August for my fiftieth birthday. I explained that when I turned twenty-five I had a big bash in New York City as I thought twenty-five was monumental, and now I wanted to do the same.

"Think about all that happened to you in the past twenty-five years. All that you've accomplished in that time," Sara said.

"Honestly, sweetie, I don't think I've accomplished anything. I want to do so much more in my life. My biggest enemy is the clock."

"Well, what have you enjoyed the most over those years?"

"The challenges, adventures, and doing things with the people I love."

"Honey, then put as much of THAT on your plate as you can over the next twenty-five years. *Time is going fast. Load your plate up with the things you love to do*."

Roger that.

Anyway, I'm excited for tomorrow.

I'm not packing for good because I want to come back to the monastery and see how I feel.

NEW YORK CITY here I come!

DAYS 14 & 15
Reentry: Back to the Madness

*"In the midst of movement and chaos, keep stillness
inside of you."*

—DEEPAK CHOPRA

In the morning, right on time, Alfredo came to pick me up.
Alfredo is our regular driver when Sara and I are in New York.
He's been with us for so long, we would mourn if he ended up
switching careers or moving away. We love him. He drove up the
driveway going about two miles per hour. Alfredo never drives at
two miles per hour. As he got closer, I could see his face though
the windshield. He was looking around like he had just driven
through some magical portal and entered into a mystical land.
It was like he just found himself in a Disney movie—enchanted
and lost in his own world. I waved but couldn't get his attention.
Once he parked, I rolled my bag over.

"Man," he said opening his car door. "Is anyone alive up
here?"

"This is how it is all the time," I said. "We're in the boonies."

"Nah-man-nah," he said. "This isn't the boonies. This is the
loonies."

"Did you bring any smoothies?"

He flashed the smile of a drug dealer and popped the trunk. I threw my bag in. When we got in he pulled out a bag of four grown-man smoothies. I finished the first one before we even buckled up. I'd been trying to convince myself that the monastery food was great, but after a few sips, I remembered how much I love smoothies.

Alfredo slammed the shift into drive and pulled out of the parking lot. I silently gazed out my window as we drove away. It was pleasantly quiet with the only sound being the snow and branches that crunched underneath our tires. As I gazed out the window I began to feel a little sad. I'd walked the monks' private road dozens of times but now; as I was leaving, I realized just how beautiful it was. Eventually, Alfredo broke the silence.

"How long have the monks been here?" he asked.

When I told him he was shocked.

"Impossible," he said. "Come on, man. Fifty years?"

As we got to the bottom of the hill, we rolled past the two mobile homes and the dogs went nuts as usual. Alfredo stomped on the gas, and we peeled out of monk road. Immediately I spotted two bike riders. And it was like seeing the ocean for the first time. I couldn't believe it. Humans! Real, non-monk humans! I kept my eye on them until they disappeared from view.

The plan was to stop at my Connecticut house on the way back to New York City to pick up my friend Mike Young. Mike is a movie director, and he's like family to us. Last April he asked if he could stay with us for a short weekend in our apartment in Manhattan while looking for a place to rent. He was shooting a film, and his production company was in the process of finding him a spot to bunk while filming. I'm not sure what happened to the rental because he stayed in our apartment for five months. My son Lazer thinks Mike is his real uncle. Mike's also a stand-up comic and one of the funniest guys I know. He once told me this joke:

"Guy's on a job interview and the interviewer says to him, 'What's your worst attribute?' And the guy says, 'I'm brutally honest.' And the interviewer says, 'I don't think that's a bad attribute.' And the guy says, 'I don't give a fuck what you think.'"

I was really looking forward to seeing Mike. I needed a laugh.

The farther we got away from the monastery the more I realized I was back in the world I'd left. As I watched the trees, mile markers, and road signs flash by, a feeling of inner happiness came over me. I felt different—lighter. I could see my reflection in the window, and there was a smile on my face. I was proud of myself for sticking it out and being open to such a different experience.

Eventually we pulled into my driveway in Connecticut. Alfredo and I had said very few words to each other. That's not usually the case, and he was looking at me oddly.

"You okay?" he asked.

"I don't think I've ever been better."

Mike piled into the car, and we headed to the city. It was great to get caught up, but as soon as we hit the interstate, Mike pulled out his phone. He started scrolling text messages, emails, and social media. I was watching him try to do all three at once. Then he started making phone calls on speaker. He kept firing through his emails as he talked to a manager about upcoming gigs. He was doing nine things at once and none of them like a monk.

"You should try monotasking," I said.

He wasn't listening, just texting and carrying on a conversation on speaker. You could get a headache watching him. Actually I kind of did, and then laughed, as he continued texting.

I really started to notice the traffic when we were about twenty miles outside of the city. We were bumper to bumper, and everyone was late for something. I imagined everyone was thinking about their next stop, next meal, or next whatever. You could see it on the faces of the drivers. The traffic only got worse. New York is like an ant farm. We climb all over one another.

It took us about an hour to get to my hotel in midtown. After Alfredo dropped me off, he was taking Mike to a friend's apartment further downtown. I wondered if he'd stay there for five months. The New York City sidewalks felt like one of those conveyor belts for people in airports. I stood there watching people and pets glide by—some coming, some going, everyone on the move—everyone gliding. I was about to grab my bag when—BAM!

I got blindsided. Pow, knocked right to the ground.

And when I looked up I saw a middle-aged guy in a suit looking down at his phone.

We just went shoulder to shoulder, and he didn't even look up.

It was like he was a bumper car at the carnival and just kept going—going—going and going.

Wow, I said to myself—was I ever that guy?

For dinner I got takeout from Rosa Mexicano. I ordered two meatless entrees, a main course vegetable plate, an order of the guacamole that they're famous for, and three corn on the cobs. I had the television on ESPN while I was stuffing my face. I was eating like a gorilla. I couldn't stop shoveling food into my face. My pace didn't slow until I started on corn cob number three.

Meanwhile, I found myself clicking from ESPN to Sports Channel to YES and back to ESPN. But after fourteen days without it, TV felt like an invasion to my senses. The announcers were talking about trades, games, stats, and highlights at a rapid pace. I snapped it off and enjoyed the rest of my vegetable plate in silence. I wondered how quickly I'd slip back to my bad habits. How long would it take for my old life to swallow me whole? It might have already.

By nine o'clock, I was exhausted. I sat in the comfortable chair in my hotel room and began to meditate. As I started my rhythmic breathing, I could hear every sound: a distant car horn from the street, footsteps in the carpeted hallway, a faint electronic buzz coming from the clock on the table next to the bed. Soon I heard nothing but the rush of air in and out of my lungs. Every day at the monastery my meditation practice became stronger. By the end of fourteen days, I was able to clear my mind for ten, fifteen minutes, even more.

I think about how an entire generation of kids has been prescribed drugs for ADHD when many might be better off if they learned to meditate. Now, I know some kids need the medication that doctors prescribe, but all medication has a potential downside. ***Meditation has no downside. Worst case is you'll miss fifteen minutes of television.***

The next morning I woke up early without an alarm. I slipped out of bed and went to the bathroom. In the mirror I got a good look at myself for the first time in two weeks. I must have lost fifteen pounds at the monastery. With my scraggly beard and emaciated body I looked like Tom Hanks in *Cast Away*. I washed my face and brushed my teeth. And when I made my way back to bed I instinctively went to cover my ears.

The BELLS...and then I looked at my phone, yup, it was 7:15 a.m. Wow—I have an internal clock. My thoughts shifted to the monks filing into the church. I wondered if they were looking over at my empty pew.

The hotel I was staying at wasn't far from Central Park, so I decided to walk the six-mile park loop. It felt right to walk, not run. The bellhop opened the door, and I reentered the chaos. There were beeping taxis, dump trucks backing up, and a street noise soundtrack playing in the background. It was coming from everywhere—surround sound. Almost every single person was on their phone. I guess I've noticed that before but never as clearly.

Now I was on high alert for someone to bump into me. I navigated my way to the opening of the park without any more injuries. On my walk I popped into the old building where Sara and I used to live on Central Park West. As I did, I saw Carlton, one of the doormen.

"Hey, man," I said. "How are you?"

"Can I help you?" Carlton asked.

"Nah," I said. "I'm here just to say hi."

"Hi to who?"

"To you," I said. "Hi, Carlton."

"Um hi," he said.

It dawned on me that he had no idea who I was. He'd never seen me bald or with a beard.

"It's Jesse."

"Holy shit," he said. "I didn't even recognize you!"

We chatted it up for a bit, and then he asked what I was doing. He wanted to know if I was okay. He kept asking. Are you okay—are you okay? And the truth was I felt great—really great. After about five minutes I took off and went to see my friend Bryan Fried.

Bryan's been one of my closest friends forever. Sara calls him one of my "Super Friends." I used to run with a group of friends in the park every Wednesday, and we called our group the "Wonderful Wednesdays," but Sara called us the "Super Friends," and he's part of that crew.

I hadn't seen Fried in a while, and I was really looking forward to catching up. I wanted to share my experience at the monastery. It was a nice five-minute walk to where he was waiting for me in the Sheep Meadow where we'd planned to meet. When I saw him I strolled up with a big smile, but he gave me the Heisman. He was deep into a conversation on his phone.

"One second," he mouthed. "Love you, brother, but I have to take this call."

Bryan was a finance guy but wasn't happy. He quit and started his own specialty contracting business. He had no prior experience or expertise in his new trade, but he followed his instinct and had the confidence he'd figure it all out if he just started. I'm super proud of him for that. He called me up when he was first putting the business plan together.

"I want to call it Elite Closets."

"You're only doing closets?"

"No, we're going to put in cabinets, shelving, and lots of stuff."

"Name sounds like you only do closets."

"Yeah, I guess it does. I've been thinking of making a change."

I suggested "WoodMasters" so to not pigeonhole him into just a closet company. He agreed and WoodMasters was born. And from the looks of it—they were super busy. Even from a few feet away I could tell he was putting out a fire.

Then he rested the phone between his neck and shoulder and whispered that he'd be off in a minute. I sat on a bench and watched. He paced back and forth; it sounded like he was arguing with someone. Finally he motioned me to come with him, I got up, and we started walking the lower loop. Eventually he ended the call and stopped to give me a hug.

"Wow," he said, stepping back and looking at me. "Are you okay?"

"I'm good, man," I said. "I'm good."

"You look kind of...scrawny."

His phone rang. He looked at the caller ID and picked it up.

"I'll call you back in twenty," he said and clicked off.

As soon as he hung up, the phone rang again. As I watched him, I was looking at so many of our lives. That's how we operate all day long. As far as picking a place to reenter the human race after a monastery stay, Manhattan might not have been the best choice. In no time, I felt the peace I'd accumulated leaking out of me like steam from a radiator. And I wasn't helping matters. My podcast started at 2:45, and I was pitching a business idea to Samsung on a conference call at 1:30. And in between I wanted to go for a steam. Too much to do, but the steam was nonnegotiable. Once Bryan and I completed the lower loop, we said our goodbyes.

Alfredo picked me up with Mike Young in the car around 1:15, and we headed to the bathhouse. I figured I'd take the Samsung call in the car to give me the most sauna time possible. But the call went late, and by the time I got off it was after 2:00.

"We're going to have to speed-sauna," I said to Mike.

The Russian & Turkish Baths have been around since the 1890s. It's now owned by two Russian guys, Boris and Dave, who had a fierce argument years ago and have had nothing to do with each other ever since. Rather than sell the bathhouse after their fight, they decided to divide the club into two groups. If you buy a membership with Dave you can't go on Boris's days, and if you buy one from Boris you can't go on Dave's. If you're neutral, like me, you just buy day passes and you can go anytime. The place is dirty, but it's what I like to call "clean dirty," just clean enough to pass code.

The bath house is really one of a kind, and over the years it has drawn it's share of celebs. Frank Sinatra was a regular customer as was John Belushi, who once said it was the only place he could find peace. It's down in the basement of an old tenement building. There's no air. And once you check in, they give you paper shorts to wear, and topless women walk around but it feels totally normal. Today you're just as likely to be sharing a sauna with a Ford model as with an eighty-year-old Russian Jewish guy or a Brooklyn boxer looking to lose weight. Like Belushi, I go to the baths just to get away from the rat race for a while.

Plus, I like to play a game to test my mental toughness. I pretend the sauna is a competition to see who can last the longest. Now I'm not talking about your average Equinox or LA Fitness sauna box. They call the hot sauna at the Tenth Street Baths the "Russian Radiant Heat Room." It feels illegally hot. New York State law stipulates that a sauna cannot be over 175 degrees, but the one at the Russian & Turkish Baths seems at least 20 degrees hotter. It's so hot that when you exit the sauna, you have to walk in slow motion to the door or your skin will feel like it's burning off.

Mike and I walked into the Radiant Room in our paper shorts, and the scorching heat immediately attacked our skin. "Holy shit, it's hot as fuck in here," Mike said.

There were two other dudes in there, a super fit actor guy who looked like he belonged in a soap opera role and a thick Russian with tattoos, a beard, and a felt hat. He was wearing a hat! Right away I knew who my competition was for the "who will leave the sauna first" game.

I was right. After about six minutes, the actor guy started mumbling and poured a bucket of ice water over himself. It didn't help. He was out the door moments later. I wasn't really worried about Mike Young either. As expected, a minute later, he said, "Yo J, this is brutal. I'm going to go jump in the cold plunge."

Which left just me and the Russian. Mano a mano.

This Russian dude was focused. He was staring at his feet in silence as the sweat dripped like a hose from his forehead. It was like the bathroom faucet was leaking from between his eyes. Drip... drip...drip onto the wood bench of the sauna. He was unwavering— just staring down at his sandals. I tried to meditate, get my mind off of the Russian and the heat. I wanted to win. But meditation in the Radiant Room was impossible. I'm not sure if a master monk could have handled the heat. It felt like my eyelids were melting.

Meanwhile, the Russian started grunting, rhythmically, like doing some type of tribal sauna breathing technique to extend his time. It sounded like it was coming from a place of strength— not weakness. I needed to pull some type of maneuver or I was going to lose. I figured I couldn't stand more than two more minutes. I better try to get him out of his trance soon.

So I went for it...

"Pretty hot, huh?" I said, trying to get him out of his zone and bring the heat to the forefront of his attention. He stopped grunting and looked right at me. With his felt hat and beard he looked like he should be riding a camel in the Sahara.

"Nah, my freeend, it's nooot preeeety hot," he said with a Russian accent. "It's foookin hot in here."

This guy was a sauna beast.

"How long do you stay in here?" I asked.

"Until I can't foookin take it anymore."

"Got it. Well, can I ask what the hat is for then?"

"The hat? Ahh, it's so the FOOOKIN roots of my hair don't burn off."

"The roots of your hair?"

"Yes. The heat will rise. Your head is up high. You're FOOOKIN roots are on your head."

No shit, Vladimir Einstein.

The Russian guy looked down after that, and the sweat rained off his body like a tropical storm. Foook that, I thought. I headed for the exit. I was out—I lose. I got a ways to go yet.

An hour later I was doing the Spartan Up podcast with Joe De Sena, the CEO and founder of the Death Race and the Spartan Race. The races include obstacles with the lengths varying from three miles to a marathon. They also hold a series of races on military bases. Joe's a trainer, fitness expert, and bestselling author. He's an animal. He's competed in ultramarathons and other long-distance events. One year he competed in fifty ultra-events and fourteen Ironmans.

Joe's extreme. I love extreme.

We met at a small restaurant on the Lower East Side of Manhattan. I got there about five minutes early and Joe was already setting up. When I entered he walked up to greet me carrying his kettlebell. He placed the kettlebell on the floor before he almost hugged last night's Mexican food out of me. The guy carries around a forty-five-pound kettlebell everywhere he goes—he even brought it on a trip to Japan—and had a kung fu master train his one-year-old son. He told me he does it as a reminder of how comfortable his life is. Once he was situated it was go time.

As we began the podcast, Joe asked me the questions I think everybody will be asking about my stay at the monastery: Why did you go? What did you miss most? What was it like? What did you get out of it?

It turned out Joe was a great interviewer. He asked a lot of straightforward questions, but he got into the nitty gritty of mental toughness and drive. He could see how this adventure was outside of my skill set since it focused more on slowing down than toughing it out. After an hour we wrapped the interview and I was on my way.

In no time I was back in Alfredo's car heading north. I punched "New Skete Monastery" into the GPS. It told us the trip would take four hours and twenty-two minutes.

I was heading back for my last day.

DAY 16

I'm Going Home Mother Monker

"Cowards never start. The weak never finish. Winners never quit."

—UNKNOWN

I got back to the monastery late last night—late in monk time. By 10:00 p.m. all the monks were asleep. Monasteries are pretty quiet all the time, but at night it's disturbingly quiet. It must be clear consciences. In some ways it felt like I was sneaking in because it was so serene. I was tiptoeing around the place. When I was in high school, my friends would tell me stories about sneaking into their houses when they got home late. There was no sneaking in my house. It didn't matter what time I came home, as long as I came home, and my mom was always waiting on the couch. All personnel had to be accounted for.

I think it was about 10:30 p.m. when I finally got settled. For my first two weeks at the monastery I was already in bed by that time. But in just one and a half days away my circadian rhythm was back to its old routine. It's not like I was bouncing off the walls like a kid with cake breath jacked up on Coca-Cola, but I was a little fidgety.

I packed for the morning. This time I'm leaving for good. Since I never really unpacked, it didn't take long to stuff the few items I had lying around into my bag. All the fruit and vegetables were gone, so one whole suitcase was going home empty. I don't know why I didn't leave from the City yesterday. Maybe I wanted to make sure I'd gotten from the monastery what I needed. Maybe I needed one more day to make it feel more "honest" and say a proper good-bye. That was necessary.

When I sent out the social media blast for book suggestions before I came up here, one of the books someone mentioned was *A Man's Search for Meaning* by Viktor Frankl. I had already read it a long time ago. At night, I had to use a reading glass because of the poor light in the cell, but I read the book twice more during my stay. Frankl wrote it in 1946. He had survived the Auschwitz concentration camp mostly by figuring out what his why was. Most of his fellow prisoners who gave up their will to live had lost their why. Frankl speaks of identifying a positive purpose and creating strong imagery around that outcome. It's a life-changing book, and the lessons can be applied to any life and circumstance. **If your why is big enough, the how usually emerges. A big why crushes smaller obstacles every time.**

I remember when Brother Christopher asked me about my why. Why was I at the monastery? I didn't have an authentic answer. I didn't want to tell him it was only about writing a book. But now, having spent two weeks with the monks, maybe I have a deeper why.

For a good portion of my stay I was figuring out my why, which I think is perfectly acceptable. But I'm not sure if I'd have gotten as much out of it if Brother Christopher hadn't posed the initial question. It echoed in my thoughts throughout my stay and made me push harder. I think it's a question I need to continually ask myself...why?

In business, you ask how and how much. Rarely why. But without a strong why we're lost, and the why often hides itself. My wife always reminds me that most advertisers talk about the "what" of a product and not the why. "This is a vacuum and it does XYZ," but they don't ever really talk about why you need it or why it was created or why it's different then everything else in the market. It's the why that makes the customer more invested in your product and more emotionally connected.

But no one needs to ask me why I'm going home.

After service, I took pictures with the monks. We hugged it out, and I must have thanked them thirty-seven times, and they kept thanking me. I took photos with everyone except Lenny. He doesn't do photos, he told me. As a going-away gift, I gave all the monks Atlanta Hawks jerseys. They tried them on and pretended to shoot hoops. Hilarious. It looked nothing like a game of basketball. More like they were swatting flies.

And then I spent an hour cleaning my cell. I swept, mopped the floor with an old towel, and washed the garbage can. It looks exactly like it did two weeks ago when I arrived. I wanted to make sure I said good-bye to Josh the Cook too. He was amazing and did me a solid smuggling in newspapers. When he reached his hand out to shake, I slipped $300 into his palm as a thank-you. At first he refused, but after I explained he could use it to treat his young daughter to something he obliged.

Money—money—money...I've learned that money can be a real awkward instrument. It changes relationships. When you don't have any, you can be perceived one way—and when you have a lot of it, you can be perceived in another. It can be intimidating and defining. My mother always used to say: "Don't ever borrow money and don't ever lend it. It will only cause problems. If you want to gift it, that's fine, but remember it's a gift."

She couldn't have been more right. Her one exception to the lending rule was to family.

Lastly, I pulled Brother Christopher to the side. I wanted to thank him for everything he'd done. He made my experience. I gave him the best hug I could. And I felt a spiritual connection. But there was something I also really wanted to ask.

"So," I said. "After I get home and talk with my wife, is it okay if I call you and put our name in for a dog?"

"Of course," he said. "You'd be a fantastic dog owner."

"Any shot we could get bumped up on the waiting list? You know, as a friend of the monks."

"Nope."

"Yeah, didn't think so," I said. "But without asking you'll never get. You'll be hearing from me. Love you, man."

Okay then... it's time to close this journal and walk out of my cell for the last time. This is it.

I'll write more when I get on the plane.

Two hours later...

We got to the airport around 11:35 a.m. I felt calm. I'm excited to see my wife and kids, but it feels very peaceful in and around me. That is until I realized I'd turned my phone off when I meditated this morning. So I flipped it back on and walked into the terminal.

Once it powered up, the emails, texts, and social media alerts started coming through in rapid fire. One after another, nonstop. It was too much, so I flipped my phone to vibrate and kept walking. Once I checked in I made my way over to security. I put a cheesecake box and pancake mix I got from the nuns on the moving black conveyor belt and walked through the X-ray machine. That's when the TSA agent stopped the belt.

"What's in the paper bag?" he asked.

"It's cheesecake and pancake mix."

"Cheesecake huh. Pancake mix, hmm. So you say. From where?" he said.

"The nuns in New Skete."

"You visited the nuns of New Skete?"

"Yes, I lived with the monks for a couple of weeks. I'm just leaving now," I said in a soft, almost biblical tone as I stared deep into his eyes.

The change in his attitude was remarkable. It was almost as though he wanted to kneel.

"Go right by, sir," he said without checking the bag.

The cheesecake moved through the X-ray machine without interruption. I could feel the other TSA agents, and the rest of the people on line, looking at me with reverence, as if I were a priest. I felt ALL WISE and shit. I had a beard and shaved head...I looked the part. As I got to the other side of the conveyor belt I was met with smiles and offers of help. Funny. Just saying the words "New Skete" transformed me from a potential drug smuggler to a holy man. The security people treated me like I might be able to help them get into heaven or something.

"New Skete." The words are magical.

What a journey. I did it!

Back at Kate's Office

"When there is no vision, there is no hope."
— GEORGE WASHINGTON CARVER

I'm heading back to Hachette Book Group. Kate is reading my diary while I take an extended lunch break. She told me to come back in a couple of hours. It's been two and a half. I have no idea what she's going to say or think. But the one thing I've got going for me is that it's honest. The diary is the most authentic version of my experience.

When I get back into the building and up to the fifth floor, I see Kate sitting in the conference room. Okay then...it's the moment of truth. I push open the door and she turns to look up at me. She's smiling. I take the seat across from her. The diary is sitting in front of her, and it looks like she's read the whole thing. I wait for her to say something—anything.

But nothing comes. It's like she's gathering her thoughts. I keep waiting.

"If we're playing who talks first loses, you aren't going to win, Kate. I'm trained in silence."

"Ha. I think it's great," she says. "There's a lot we can do with this."

"Really?"

"Yes, just as with *SEAL*, I think people are going to want to live vicariously through your experience. They're going to want to uncover some of the benefits you received from your time with the monks. Things they can apply to their daily lives."

"What do you mean?"

"Well, whenever someone mentions they read *Living with a SEAL*, they usually comment about the 40 percent rule," she says.

"When you think you're done, you're only at 40 percent of what your body is capable of doing," I interrupt.

"That's powerful," she says. "And it really resonated with readers."

"I agree, and I've heard that reaction, too," I say. "If people can access that extra 60 percent, it can make a significant impact on their life. And just knowing the 60 percent exists can be the difference between finishing and not finishing."

"Exactly," Kate says. "So we need more of that in this book."

"I get it, but I feel like this book isn't as funny as *SEAL*."

"Not every book has to be funny. It has to be genuine," she says. "And I think we need to share with the reader what you learned."

"Like monk wisdom?"

"Yes," she says. "What you learned from being up there, or perhaps things you already knew that this experience strengthened. We need to offer something readers can apply to their daily lives. You know—the takeaways. We want the reader to be able to feel the way you felt when you left the monastery. Things such as Remember Tomorrow are great. I really like that one. That's why people are going to buy your book. And it's your job to deliver."

"Roger that."

PART III
Ten Real-World Benefits

One of many long walks.

1. #ItsNotJustaHose

"There is nothing so fatal to character
as half-finished tasks."
—DAVID LLOYD GEORGE

As I left Kate's office I thought back on my trip. One of the biggest takeaways from my experience is how much effort the monks put into the small things. Things like making their beds, doing the dishes, and sweeping the floors were given maximum effort. There's an old adage: "How you do anything is how you do everything." It's the small things you do during the day that build your character and grit. It's the small things you do that are indications of what you're becoming.

As I mentioned, there are various studies pointing to the fact that grit is the number one indicator of future success. **So if we could all be a little more "gritty," then we'd all be a bit more successful** in all the buckets of our lives. Well, how do we do it?

When I got home from the monastery I was playing with my son Lazer outside in our backyard. I had a freezing cold hose flowing and was trying to spray him as he ran back and forth. Ten minutes into our game Sara yelled for us to come inside for dinner.

After one last spray to the face when my son wasn't looking, I dropped the hose and ran toward the house. I had a full-blown conversation in my head as I headed inside. I told myself it was okay to leave the hose lying on the ground instead of cleaning it up and putting it on the hanger. "I'll just do it later," I told myself.

No big deal, right?

Wrong.

That isn't just a hose. That's a reflection of what I am to be. By leaving the hose on the ground and telling myself it's okay and I'll do it later, I'm really telling myself, "Maybe someone else will do it for me" or "It's okay to not finish what I started" or "I'll put it off until tomorrow." I'm basically creating an environment in my head that says it's okay to be lazy, it's okay to not be a finisher, it's okay to put things off.

Those little moments happen multiple times a day for us all. It's these small things that the monks excelled at. There was not an ounce of laziness or procrastination at New Skete. **By consistently doing things you may not want to do, you create an environment in your head that says you're okay doing hard things.** You're training yourself to go through obstacles rather than let them deter you. The other side of the conversation in my head was saying: Jesse, pick up the hose, roll it in in a circle, and put it on the hanger. Finish what you started. Complete the task. You're a finisher. How you do anything is how you do everything. It's not just a hose.

So I marched back outside, coiled the hose, and put it away properly. I felt good. The backyard looked clean. My shit was in order. I stood there for a moment admiring my backyard. And then SPLAT!

A perfectly thrown water balloon delivered from my son smacked me in the head.

Well played, Lazer, well played.

With Brother Stavros.

2. #28470Days

"Time is what we want the most, but what we use worst."

—WILLIAM PENN

One of the first things I became aware of on Day 1 was my relationship with time. I had hints of it on Mount Washington, but sitting in my cell on the first night, I quickly figured out I was going to be there for a total of 1,286,000 million seconds, and it freaked me out. I realized I had a lot of time on my hands. Or did I?

The average American male lives to be about seventy-eight years old, and I'm forty-nine at the writing of this book. That means if I'm average, I have about 10,495 days left. Since I sleep roughly one-third of those days I really have 7,871 days. That's nothing, that's only twenty-nine summers...and I LOVE SUMMERS!

When we think about relationships we often think in terms of people. How is our relationship with our parents, friends, spouses, kids? **We rarely think about our relationship with time, and for many of us (myself included) that relationship is often out of balance.**

I started to do some math, and it put time in perspective. My parents are eighty-eight years old, and I see them about four times a year. Well, if they live to be ninety-two (I hope they live much longer), then that would mean I only have sixteen more times to see them. That's unacceptable. When you put time in perspective, you realize what's important and you reprioritize things. I immediately booked a flight to see them.

The monastery was a huge hourglass. When you sit in your cell for hours at a time with silence and no distractions, you realize how slowly time can go. But when you live in the big city and live superfast, you often look up one day and your kids are all grown, and that's when you realize how fast time has gone.

How many days do you have left? How do you want to spend them? And whom do you want to spend them with? As I get older these are the questions that become more and more important to me and I continue to gain an appreciation for urgency.

"If you can't live longer, live deeper."—Italian proverb

3. #TheBestHaveaProcess

"Plans are worthless, but planning is everything."
—DWIGHT D. EISENHOWER

While I was shadowing the monks at the dog training center, it became eminently clear I was around greatness. The monks of New Skete are among the best in the world at dog training. It's not up for debate. And watching it firsthand was fascinating. The dogs arrived for their first day of training as complete misfits and left valedictorians of doggy school.

One thing I knew before I ever stepped foot on the monastery was *if you're surrounded by greatness—take notes, pay attention, and ask questions.* I learned this by accident. Twenty-five years ago I assumed what it took to be a great musician was different from what it took to be a great chef or great gymnast. I didn't think there was a blueprint for greatness. But I was wrong.

In 2001, my partner and I started a private jet card company called Marquis Jet. It wasn't easy, but we grew the company to the largest private jet card company in the world. And despite the success, the greatest gift Marquis Jet ever gave to me was being around so many people who were the best in the world at what they do. We flew all-star athletes, the most successful entrepreneurs, and world-renowned doctors. I spent hours up in the air with them, chatting and picking their brains.

I'd always ask them about their daily routines: "What do you do first thing in the morning?" or "How do you manage your time?" I wanted to gain insight into what makes the greatest in their fields tick. It was during these discussions I uncovered several traits that so many of these industry leaders had in common. For starters, virtually all of them developed a process that works best for them over time. SEAL has a process. Warren Buffett has a process. The Rolling Stones have a process. And the monks definitely have a process similar to all of the other greats I've ever interacted with. Here's a glimpse of theirs:

A. **The monks get up early.** The day started before sunrise. By the time I greeted them in church for the morning service, most of them had already tended to their dogs, meditated, and reviewed their tasks for the day. When I asked Brother Stavros why they do this, he told me the one race he ALWAYS likes to win is the race against the sun rising. Like so many of the greats in every field, mornings are magical for the monks. When I got home I started getting up around 5:00 a.m. and going for quiet jogs. There was never anybody outside in my neighborhood in the early morning. I'd take pride in what I was doing and say to myself, "There are 7 billion people on earth, and I'm the only one up and on these streets."

Beat the sun. Beat your competition. Try it.

B. **The monks have a plan.** Every night before they went to sleep they wrote a plan for the next day. They were organized. They prioritized the important things that had to get done first and focused on completing those tasks until they went on to the next. There was no guessing as to what had to get done that day; every day had a plan, and the plan had to be executed. I hear this theme a lot: "A goal without a plan is just a wish."

C. **The monks are efficient.** There was very little dilly-dallying during the day. Time was sacred. I didn't see any small talk or chatter around the monastery. The monks executed with a focus that was laser sharp. I think about all the time I've spent in the gym talking to my trainer or walking around thinking about what I have to do next. If I added all that wondering time up, it'd equal weeks of wasted downtime. The monks maximized the day.

D. **The monks don't get flustered.** When Brother Stavros's car got stuck in the snow there was no panic. Nobody called AAA to come help. The monks circled everyone up, and we pushed the car out of the snow. While it may not seem like a big deal, it's the way they approached the problem that struck me as noteworthy. They were calm and deliberate in all their problem solving. Nobody was mad, upset, or frustrated. They had to fix the problem and worked as a team to get it done. One theme I've seen in so many of the great entrepreneurs, parents, and coaches is they don't panic. They operate well under pressure.

Movie night with the monks.

4. #HappinessTest

"Happiness isn't something you experience; it's something you remember."

—OSCAR LEVANT

Within the first thirty minutes of stepping foot on the monastery, Brother Christopher asked me if I was happy. And I felt pretty confident that happiness was not one of the things I was searching for at the time. I had it already. I am happy. (A friend recently told me that I was the happiest person he'd ever met.) But Brother Christopher also said something that resonated. He believes too many people wittingly or unwittingly constrict their happiness.

"Wouldn't it be wonderful if there was no lid on happiness?" he asked.

Yes—yes, it would be.

So he got me thinking. How do you lift the lid on happiness?

Just after he'd won the Nobel Prize, Albert Einstein was staying at a hotel in Japan. When the bellboy brought up his luggage he realized he didn't have any money. So he found a piece of scrap paper and wrote his theory of how to have a happy life. He handed it to the bellboy as a tip. The note read: "A calm and modest life brings more happiness than the pursuit of success combined with constant restlessness."

In this day and age living calmly is a lot easier said than done. What I learned from the monks is that **you can find calmness during your day and small doses of calmness can open a door to happiness**. And with all due respect to Albert E., I think that you can pursue happiness just as you pursue success.

Not too long ago, I was preparing for a speech I had to give. I was basically writing it in my head while I ran ten miles. Somewhere around mile three I started to wonder if there was a scale to gauge happiness. There are myriad ways to measure other key areas of our lives: weight is measured by stepping on a scale, income measured by a tax bracket, an IQ test for intelligence, but there's no simple way to quantify happiness.

With each stride the idea developed. **We spend endless hours doing things that make us happy but invest much less time working on changing the things that make us unhappy**. I'd much rather watch a football game (which makes me happy) than tackle difficult issues about myself (which can make me unhappy).

So later that night, I was onstage in front of 1,000 highly successful people. These were folks who owned their own businesses and had a high net worth. On paper this pool of people would most likely check the happiness box. So I posed this question:

"Think about all the buckets in your life: your health, your relationships, work, finances, etc., EVERYTHING. Now, on a scale of 1–10, with the Dalai Lama being a 10 out of 10 on the happiness scale and the guy who's at rock bottom being a 1, what is your happiness number?"

After thirty seconds I said, "No need to put any one person on the spot; let's do it this way. Everyone who is a 7 or less, please stand up."

Remarkably, almost everyone in the room rose to their feet.

A thousand highly successful CEOs and industry leaders scored themselves a 7 or less.

"A 7 out of 10 sounds pretty good, right?" I said into the microphone. "But if your child came home with a 70 on their math test, that's a C–. If you're number was a 6, that's 60 percent and that's an F in the most important bucket of your life—happiness."

I was shocked how so many people in the audience initially seemed perfectly content with a 7. They didn't realize they were going through life under indexing in this category. What's amazing about this test, however, is not your score but what you identify by doing it. When you take this test your brain automatically starts at a 10. It wants you to be happy. Then it immediately subtracts the two to three biggest things in your life that are making you unhappy. Try it.

The issues contributing to your unhappiness literally appear in your head—automatically. It can be anything: being overweight, having no money, an unhealthy relationship, a crappy job. The first two to three things that popped into your head are the things blocking you from being happier. Remove one, and your happiness grades out at a B. Remove two, and you go to the top of the class. Identifying what keeps you from being happier is the first step. When you begin working to remove the obstacles, you are taking the next steps to an A+.

I already knew what made me happy (family, working out, challenging myself), but by meditating, monotasking, and otherwise clearing the clutter in my mind, the monks taught me how to see what made me unhappy (too many distraction and intrusions, infringements on my time), and that showed me what I needed to change. Identify and improve, identify and improve. It's kind of simple if you just allow it, but it starts with the one question Brother Christopher asked me: "Are you happy?"

5. #DodgetheArrows

"Do it over and over again until it becomes part of who you are."

—UNKNOWN

Interestingly, one of the best things I learned wasn't from one of the monks, it was from a dog. Remember when I was trying to distract Rainbow while she was being trained? Like most of us, Rainbow was easily distracted when she started her training. Her natural inclination was to react to whatever stimuli she encountered on her path. A squirrel runs by, and every fiber in her furry body wants to dart after it. Another dog? How in the hell can you expect her to pass that up? Her reaction is instinctual, but not all instincts are helpful.

Brother Thomas trained Rainbow to completely ignore the interferences coming her way that may distract from her goal. "I'm training the dog to block out the noise and keep going," he explained. This isn't unlike our own lives where **most of our goals get shattered because we don't block out the noise.** We're not trained to ignore the distractions. We listen to naysayers, we get pulled in multiple directions and sidetracked by trivial things. And ultimately, if enough of those distractions pile up, we fall short of our goals.

In my life, I call my distractions "arrows," and I didn't realize how bombarded I was by them until I stepped away from it all. I realized how under attack I am DAILY. On any given day, I'm dodging unessential requests for my time, my own negative thoughts, and life's circumstances. And they come from all directions.

I find that many of the personal requests we get are one-sided agendas—people who want something from us. Don't get me wrong, I've been on that side of the equation and imposed on people to help me get ahead in life. I know the importance of making connections. And I also understand the importance of helping those behind you on the ladder to success. But if you say yes to too many of those requests, it takes time away from your goals.

The arrows also fly toward us in personal challenges. Say you are training for a race and your training plan calls for early morning runs. Well, it's cold in the morning, it may be snowing, it's dark outside—those are all arrows. Those are reasons to NOT get out there. It's important that when these arrows appear you acknowledge them for what they are. One of the keys to accomplishing a big goal is to avoid the obstacles. Dodge the arrows.

Lastly, there are the arrows that come at you as part of everyday life. Your toilet overflows, the car won't start, the boss is being a dick—again. Though these distractions might be unavoidable, they don't have to deter you from your goal. Sometimes the arrows are things that you don't have: you want to take a vacation, but you don't have the money; you want to start a business, but you don't have the experience; or you want to take a class, but you don't have the time. These types of arrows stop you dead in your tracks. But they don't have to. ***Rainbow doesn't stop walking because she doesn't own any food. She just keeps on going and has the faith there's food somewhere down the line.***

When I watched Rainbow walk with Brother Thomas there was no denying she was happy. Her whole body sprang with purpose. But learning to not react to something so instinctual took practice and wasn't easy. If you have a goal, don't get caught up in the distractions. ***You have to shut off all the noise coming at you to be successful.*** Rainbow had to train like a dog, and so do we.

Best buddies.

6. #GoWhereYou ThinkBest

"Thinking: the talking of the soul with itself."
— PLATO

I believe thinking is a lost art form. Today, we get answers on demand from Google, Siri, and Alexa (if you're listening to this in audio format, Alexa probably just turned herself on). But many of us don't invest any real time into thinking. Yet, giving ourselves time to think is one of the best investments we can make—and there's no risk.

The night when Brother Christopher told me to think for the next twelve hours, I was at a loss. At the time my "thinking" was a scattershot process that took up too much of my mental energy. I was overwhelmed. But over the course of two weeks I thought about thinking, mostly because I was forced into it—there was little else to do.

I found myself alone for a lot of my stay. But in the real world, I have to find time to be alone, and I have to find a place I'm comfortable alone—a place where I like to be alone. If I don't exercise my thinking muscle, it goes away and I don't think clearly.

My wife thinks best in her car. We live two miles from

her office, which is a ten-minute drive, but Sara has created a forty-minute "fake commute" so she can think (I wonder if she thought of that idea while driving in the car?). She's set up cameras in her vehicle so she can say all of her thoughts out loud while driving and not worry about forgetting them.

For me, it's running or walking. I recently calculated I've run almost every day for the past twenty-five years, almost 36,000 miles, which is like walking around the circumference of the earth one and a half times. That's like 9,000 hours alone. It's when I do my best thinking—pounding the pavement or the path or the track. Without it, I don't think I'd have had nearly the same success in my life. It's like a forced meditation for me. That's why I choose to run without music. I can clear my mind by listening to my footfalls. And usually within a few miles I'm in sync with my body and spirit. I'm totally focused and in stride with the world around me. Everything is clear.

I've come up with stuff like Halloween costumes for the family, written entire speeches for speaking engagements, solved work problems, figured out the best way to make amends, and created new ideas for business ventures—all while running. And as soon as I finish I immediately write them down in one notebook. Putting it on paper de-clutters your head and frees up energy. I've learned that **when you're in the zone, STAY THERE**! If you're thinking clearly, then keep it going—extend the session. That's when it's time to go for a longer run.

One day, not too long after I got back from the monastery, I called Turney and asked how he was doing. We went back and forth for a bit, and then he launched into how he was battling writer's block for an article he was working on. How nothing was coming to him, how he couldn't get the words on the page, and that his day was a big fat zero. He was defeated and felt like he couldn't recover.

"Turney," I said. "Where do you come up with your best ideas? Solve problems? Figure things out? Where is that?"

"Um," he said. "On the toilet."

"Well then," I said. "Sit on the fucking toilet."

He called me thirty minutes later and said—PROBLEM SOLVED!

Brother Christopher and all the other monks made me think about thinking. It's a skill, a craft, and an art. It can be worked on and improved with practice. We all have an opportunity to become better thinkers. Go where you think best, and spend more time there.

Vacuuming the guest room: Doing one thing at a time.

7. #Monotask

"The successful warrior is the average man,
with laser-like focus."
— BRUCE LEE

The first time Brother Stavros asked me to wash the dishes was after the retreat. I wanted to know what the record time was for cleaning them all.

"Work with your hands and pray with your heart," he said.

Wait, what?

I had no idea what he was talking about. And I had no time for riddles. I had dishes to do and records to break. I flipped on the water and grabbed a sponge. The monks had served lunch to over a hundred people, so I started flying. I was washing, drying, and washing, drying, and stacking like a one-man car wash assembly line. Dishes, pots, glasses, whatever they had, I was washing it. I would have washed a monk if he were standing next to me.

Every time I thought I was making progress, another monk came with a handful of dirty dishes. Then I got a cookie tray stuck, wedged in between the sinks; it was messing with my record pace. Plus, my lower back was killing me. And while I was doing the dishes, I was thinking about my afternoon chores, the time I had left, how cold it was, etc.

I was doing it wrong. I wasn't doing it like a monk.

During my stay I wondered how the monks have such great ENERGY and EFFORT. They're so EFFICIENT in EVERYTHING they do. The answer is they monotask, that's how they do it. And they do it with perfection. The monks do their job(s) with zest, but only one dish at a time. Each dish is done like the world depends on it. Maybe it does? They're completely, singularly focused. There are no distractions. **They don't increase their effort, they increase their concentration.** A task is never a race. And there's never a finish line. There is only now.

Me? I'm all over the map. I don't get the same effort. We live in a world of to-do lists. We're overwhelmed, short-circuiting, and it becomes so intimidating to get things done. Sometimes I don't know where to start and the natural reaction is to do everything. Let me try to get it all done, but I'll leave a task with a promise I'll get back to it later. When I take on a task, I want to finish it as quickly as possible so I can tackle the next. For me, everything is a race. I thought what was important was doing as much as I could in a day. **I was focused on the quantity, not the quality.**

The monks live in a world of quality. No task is left half done, and each task is done to the best of their ability. Monotasking brings better effort, results, and satisfaction. When Brother Gregory brought in another load of dishes, I asked him how many more I'd have to do.

"You only have to do one," he said. "Just the one you're holding in your hand."

For most of my adult life I've tried to be an excellent multitasker, but not anymore. Nope. I try to monotask multiple times a day.

With Brother Marc. Down 10 lbs.

8. #MakeaContractwithYourself

"When there is no enemy within, the enemies outside cannot hurt you."

—AFRICAN PROVERB

As we were hiking up a paved road and talking, Brother Thomas told me the four vows all of the monks take when they join the monastery. I'm definitely not giving up sex was my first thought when he mentioned the chastity vow. But it made me realize the importance of establishing and honoring your own nonnegotiables. And the monks' strict rules gave me the idea to have my own set of vows. So, on the last night at the monastery, I decided to **write a "contract with myself." A list of how I wanted to live my life.**

I read it to myself every morning, and it's been helpful in guiding me during the day. This exercise takes only a second, and the benefits are long lasting. Here is my contract with myself:

I'm going to thank God first thing in the morning.
I'm going to show appreciation for having this day.
Today I'm going to be the best version of me that I can be.
I'm going to try hard at whatever it is I do.

I'm going to be present and patient.
I'm going to be a teacher to my kids.
I'm going to be a good son, brother, and friend.
I'm going to be giving to my wife.

I have signed many contracts in my life, but never one with myself. It feels good to write one and even better to keep it.

9. #ExperienceIsOverrated

*"Life can only be understood backwards, but it must
be lived forwards."*

—SØREN KIERKEGAARD

It turns out the nuns built their home in 1971. They took
a woodshop class in town and learned how to construct a
house. They also made many of the desks and tables they use
on a daily basis. When I asked how they accomplished all of
that without any experience, Sister Cecilia said:

"Necessity is the mother of invention."

You know when you hear someone say something and it
feels like they knocked it out of the park? Well, at that point
I was looking at Sister Cecilia like she was Aaron Judge and
she just drove one deep over the centerfield wall in Yankee
Stadium. Wow—no truer words have been spoken. Necessity
is the mother of invention.

And the monks went into the dog breeding business
without any practical experience. In fact, the only experience
they had collectively with dogs was Kyr, the original dog they
had as a pet. And yet they were able to grow into one of the
most renowned German shepherd breeding programs in the
United States, and they went on to become world-famous

dog trainers and the authors of multiple *New York Times* bestselling dog training books. All of that—without any experience.

They're not the only ones: Richard Branson, Thomas Edison, Colonel Sanders, Rachael Ray, Abraham Lincoln, Winston Churchill, and Oprah all have something in common. They became incredibly successful in fields in which they had no experience. I could give you example after example of people in business, sports, and life who succeeded spectacularly without experience. My wife, Sara, is another great example.

How did they do it? Well, maybe **the most important ingredient to their success was they didn't waste time thinking they couldn't succeed. Negativity stops dreams.** It's like the antithesis of a dreamcatcher. Even if you're not brimming with confidence, try to keep your thoughts positive. I like to have the end of the movie (my goal) in my head and then fill in the script as I go. Even if the script requires rewrites, the goal stays the same. Act as if you're going to succeed, and chances are you will.

The monks didn't walk around saying: "I don't know anything about carpentry; I don't know how to breed dogs." What they said was, "It's a good idea to have a monastery" and "Breeding dogs would be a good way to make money." And then they just went about trying their best.

Maybe the best part of having no experience is it's quicker than getting experience! If Sara had gone to business school, studied the garment manufacturing business, and then taken a course in product labeling to come up with the name Spanx, it'd have taken her half a lifetime. And by then someone else might have come up with the idea or she might have begun to believe the negative thoughts that everyone has in their heads.

Instead, she just jumped in. When you immerse yourself in an idea you're passionate about it and on full alert, every cell of your body becomes a fully engaged receptor of the stimuli that surrounds you. It's like when SEAL had me jump into a frozen lake. I was instantly more alert than I ever had been, and my survival instincts kicked in and were razor sharp.

The other thing about entering into a new business or even a relationship without experience—you engage your instinctual drive to survive. For the monks, it was do or die. When the monks started their breeding business, they read every book on dog breeding they could get their hands on, and then they read them again. They called breeders across the country and asked for help. They did the same thing when they started training dogs. I'm convinced one of the best ways to learn is to be self-taught. You can't get away with cutting corners or slacking off when you're both teacher and student.

Experience is overrated. It takes too long. If you're moved to do something—DO IT. The last thing you need to worry about is you've never done it before. Most of us want to wait until we either have the right amount of experience or feel it's the right time to tackle something. That right time rarely comes. So yeah, when Sister Cecilia said, "Necessity is the mother of invention," I totally got it!

Josh the Cook hooked me up. It's the little things.

10. #BuildYourEdge

"The past is where you learned the lessons. The future is where you apply the lessons."
— UNKNOWN

When I left the monastery, Alfredo asked me how I felt. I assumed he was expecting a response like *focused* or *calm* or maybe even *relaxed*, but that's not what I was feeling.

"I'm proud," I said.

As we drove away I sat there strapped in the seat belt and took a long sigh. And then I smiled—a proud smile. I knew I was going home successful. I put the challenge in front of me, tried to build on it, and hung in until it was completed. I was proud I had the courage to come to the monastery, stick it out, and give my best effort.

Effort is the true source of pride—not results.

I once heard a guest on my friend Lewis Howes's podcast say that every day he wakes up and tells himself: "Today I'm going to try my hardest at everything I do." And then, at the end of each day before he goes to sleep he asks himself: "Did I indeed try my best today?" If the answer is yes to both questions, then he considers it a hell of a day. Think about it, we can't always control the outcome, the results, but we can always control our effort. I believe trying our best every day is a great way to measure success.

The monks' daily EFFORT is unrivaled, contagious, and supersuccessful. Every day is about doing the best they can regardless of the task. Do you just want to make your bed? Or do you want to make your bed like a monk? There's a big difference between the two. Once I started to really understand the monks' determination, I started to feel a shift in my thinking.

While I was at the monastery it inspired me to make a pledge to spend as much time as possible around people who are focused on effort. I want to continue pushing forward this element in my life. Effort is everything. I want to be around people who don't cut corners and feel proud at the end of each day. I may not share all of the beliefs the monks have, but you can't question their discipline. Their energy is infectious and inspiring.

And because of their EFFORT the monks have EDGE. Edge is an internal advantage. It's the right hook that your brain can use to knock out fear or that internal bully when it creeps into your thoughts. When you gain edge it's like stamping a permanent "I get shit done" tattoo on your brain. You can always access it when needed. And **you get edge by stepping into the unknown and by consistently doing things that are hard.**

My edge in life has primarily come through challenging myself physically. It's a different kind of edge than the monks'. And I'm often asked why I like challenges so much. Maybe it's because I learn something about myself every time, or maybe it's because I'm an adrenaline junkie. But when I get a good look under my own hood, I'm able to use that experience for future endeavors.

My past challenges have given me a confidence and swagger that I can't get from reading a book, listening to a speaker, or attending a conference. The challenges have taught me about accessing my own courage. The same courage it takes to start a business or quit a job or take any kind of risk.

When I pulled up to the monastery I had a nervous pit in my stomach. The same feeling I get before a big meeting or standing at the starting line of a marathon. I was scared of the unknown that was ahead. I was nervous of what could happen—what would happen. But I also knew that those same feelings meant a growth opportunity was on the horizon. And on the last day when I left I knew I had gained another layer of edge—the monks' edge.

This experience was an edge enhancer. Thanks, monks!

PART IV
The New Beginning

Don't tell Sara, but we are going on the waiting list!

Adding to My Life Résumé

After I left Kate's office I hustled to La Guardia Airport. I wanted to catch the next flight to Atlanta. The meeting with my editor was positive and productive, but I'm still not 100 percent sure I have a book. I'm missing something. And I need time to figure out what that something is. On the plane I take out a pen and my diary and flip it to a blank page and start to write.

Things I Like about Monks:

1. Monks do one thing at a time.
2. Monks don't rush. They do things slowly and deliberately.
3. Monks don't cut corners. They do it completely.
4. Monks do less...but do more.
5. Monks remain calm. They don't panic.
6. Monks are okay being alone—they thrive at it.
7. Monks study all different kinds of topics to enhance growth.
8. Monks devote time to sitting.
9. Monks smile.

10. Monks live simply.
11. Monks don't waste time.
12. Monks have a strong community and family unit.
13. Monks have a love affair with life.

The plane starts to taxi, and we slowly make our way to the runway. There's got to be a creative way to tell this story. I've got to find a monk-like way. The flight attendants make their final pass down the aisle reminding everyone to fasten their seat belts. I close my diary and put it under the seat. Eventually the captain tells us we're next for takeoff.

I have a lot of work to do, but I'm going to wait until I can go where I think best.

The next evening, I'm on a run in our neighborhood. It's unseasonably warm, so I'm thinking ten miles sounds good. As I run I begin thinking about the monks. I wonder what they're doing; they're probably in the church singing to kick off the nightly service. Lenny's probably lighting the incense. I keep running.

As my mind clears, I realize I'm focused only on the rhythmic beat of my feet slapping the concrete. Everything else has drifted away. It feels like meditating. Then, out of nowhere, the conversation with Kate replays in my thoughts. And with it comes the structure of my book. I'll just write it the same way I told her the story. That's it. The Mount Washington adventure plays in my head. I see myself with Kevin the Cop at the top of the mountain. That's it—that's it. Like most great spiritual journeys this one starts on a mountaintop. I race home.

Sweating, heart beating, still in my shorts and T-shirt, I plop down in my chair and begin to outline.

I access my inner monk and monotask. My goal is to write every day and get one chapter done a week. I create a pie chart of my twenty-four hours in a day and carve out three to four hours for writing. In that time the only thing I'm allowing myself to do is work on the book.

My office door is closed, the phone is turned off, and so is my Wi-Fi. I remove all possible and potential distractions. And at first it's just words on the page, a stream of consciousness, mixed-up thoughts and stories told out of order. But slowly the narrative starts to form. Sentences are cut, scenes are added, and the words start to take shape. The rest of the day is given to running my business and dodging arrows.

At night, when I'm not writing, I'm present with my family. It's one of my nonnegotiables. I spend time with Sara and the kids. We play board games and run around the yard like it's 1985—no distractions. And some of the time I spend with just me—on the couch watching the Hawks. It's my guilty pleasure. **I realized that if I take just one hour of personal time a day for the next thirty years, I'll gain about 11,000 hours of "me" time.** That's over one full year and a quarter of time. Imagine freeing up an entire year to do what you want.

And each day I get up and go to my office. I'm energized from my goal, and I'm committed to the process. I tell myself I'm going to make the book part of my daily routine for the duration of the goal (until it's done). It's not a chore, it's a lifestyle. Sure, some days I feel like slacking, but I have a Post-it on my computer that reads: REMEMBER TOMORROW. That always gets me through. And I'm ahead of schedule. I have the first sixty pages done in two weeks.

Just as I start to clean up my diary, I realize my experience at the monastery might be able to help others. We can all access our inner monk, slow the clock, and remove the lid on happiness. We can become better listeners. We can get more out of life. And that means go out and do things, take chances. That's what I'm doing.

But you'll have plenty of reasons not to: kids, getting older, and "I don't know what I'm doing." The excuses will pile up fast. But don't listen to those voices. Beat up the bully in your own head. And once you make up your mind to take the chance, take it right away. Turney once told me that when addicts agree to go to rehab the protocol is to immediately drive them to the airport. He said statistically that each passing hour when addicts are not on their way to rehab, the chances of them not going goes up exponentially. It's because addicts listen to all of the excuses about why they don't really need to go to rehab. I think the same thing happens to all of us sometimes. Once the moment passes, it's really hard to get it back. Urgency is our friend, and we should treat it as such.

My sixty pages shrink to forty as I cut whole sections that don't matter. It's hard to read your own writing and have an objective opinion. Some days I think it's good, and other days I think it sucks. But I need to stay focused on the task and not listen to the voice, Billy the Bully in my head that's telling me to stop or it's not any good.

The diary needs some more work, but I think it's important to keep it authentic. Authenticity over everything. I don't want to play with it too much. It needs to be a diary. I find opportunities to illuminate more and touch on thoughts that never made it to the page. I keep going.

One of the most asked questions I've gotten since returning is: Have I changed? *Into what?* **I haven't changed. I've expanded. I now have a collection of memories in my brain's photo album that I can access at any time.** I gained insight I can draw upon at any moment. So, sure, I've changed, but only in the sense of feeding my soul.

Another important gift I took is patience. Now when I have to go to some lengthy engagement or something I used to think of as a painful waste of time, it's a walk in the park. I can sit through anything for three or five hours without hesitation—long drives—no problem—five-hour layover in Detroit—easy-peasy—Catholic wedding ceremony—layup. I used to fight those moments every minute of the way. Now, I have a different appreciation for time.

In some ways this experience is similar to my experience with SEAL. Back then I reinforced a mentally tough mind-set, but with the monks I learned to develop a peaceful, serene, no-worry mind-set. I changed my spiritual diet. It helped me focus on what is truly important and realize that much of my worry is irrelevant. My experiences enhanced all situations and allow me to be present. And I can tap into it at any point during my day.

Last night my son had a fever, and we knew we were in for a long night.

"I'm so sorry I can't stay with him because I'm leaving for the airport," Sara said. "Can you do it?"

"Sorry—why are you sorry?"

It was a walk in the park. I woke our son up every hour; I checked his temperature and made sure he was alright. I probably slept a total of three hours, but not once did I think about how bad it sucked. I was grateful that I'm in a position to care for my children—it's a gift. **Being a dad is what I signed up for, and that means anything that comes along with it**. Fever is part of the process, and that's what I signed up for. But without my monk experiences, I probably wouldn't have been so carefree about it. I probably would have bitched and whined.

And by this morning, I'm happy to report, my son is already feeling better.

I take the next week to clean up my diary and write down all of my takeaways. It's the routines, habits, and mindset I learned. But it's a different kind of writing, so I have to change gears a little bit. It's not something I'm used to. I wrote primarily in a narrative form for my first book, and writing rhymes and jingles is a whole different skill set. But thankfully, no experience is required—so I just show up and write. Three weeks later I finish. It's not pretty, but it's much easier to work with than 250 blank pages.

The first draft of my book is done.

The next day I'm on my way to the local country club where I have a meeting. I'm taking a break from the book to let it breathe. I once read that Stephen King likes to hide his manuscripts in a drawer for six weeks after he types THE END, but I'm no Stephen King and I have a deadline that doesn't line up with that timetable. I pull my car into the parking lot near the front entrance, lock it, and head over.

I have an appointment or a meeting; actually I'm not sure what to call it. It's more like an interview, I guess. One thing I'm sure about is that it's not a mission. But I was asked to be part of an entrepreneurial club that has a membership. I didn't seek it out, but when they contacted me it sounded interesting—something that might be mutually beneficial. Inside the building it feels exactly like you'd expect a suburban country club to feel like—elegant architecture and the smell of old money. The vested gentleman behind the front desk directs me to the meeting room. As I make my way across the red carpet I visualize how hopping this place must be in the summer. I can see kids running around in bathing suits and men and women in golf attire. But today it's fairly empty. I pass an older couple who smile at me, and then I see a couple of business guys looking guilty for not being at work.

As I enter into the formal meeting room, I see Ted standing there. He's about my age and looks like he might have been a member of the Young Republicans Club in college. He's cleaner cut than cleaning products. I bet if you flipped him upside down he'd make a hell of a mop with that perfectly parted brown hair. Or maybe you could hang him on your rearview mirror as an air freshener. And he's so proper, with a firm handshake and pearly white teeth. I instantly feel like I know this guy. By know him, I mean I know what he likes, how he operates, and what he's looking for. The dude is all business. And he probably doesn't use the word "dude."

We sit.

He explains how the club works and what kind of

candidates they're looking for. They not only want to net-work across the country, they want to find synergies that help members succeed. It sounds like a I-got-a-guy-or-girl network, meaning that if you're a member, then you'll most likely have a trusted contact in almost every industry. I've never been in a business club before, but the more he talks about the concept the more appealing it sounds. Eventually we start to go down some side streets with personal talk. Ted is a family man; he's giving off a high ethics and moral vibe. I like him. Once he concludes his pitch, he smiles. And then he nods his head slightly up and down.

"So," Ted says. "Can I see your résumé?"

"My résumé? I don't have a résumé."

"What do you mean you don't have a résumé?" he asks. "Everyone has a résumé."

"Well, I don't. I don't believe in them."

He's looking at me like I just told him I believe the world is flat. He's so confused. And then after he gets over his shock, I tell him I don't believe in résumés in the traditional sense. **I think it's more important to have a life résumé, you know, like collecting moments, creating experiences, and doing more.** I believe that's a real indication of who you are. He doesn't disagree, so I keep going.

"Did you know that the average recruiter scans a pros-pect's résumé for only six seconds?" I say. "Six seconds. Six seconds to determine whether someone is qualified for the job. I don't know about you, but I don't think that's enough time to judge someone's life work. If people focused more time on having experiences, it'd give them more depth. It might even help them land their dream job."

"That's interesting."

"Yeah, what if we flipped the model upside down and spent more time on building our life résumé?"

"Well," Ted says. "What's your first job experience on your *life* résumé?"

"Break-dancing," I say. "I drove from Long Island to Washington, D.C., in 1985 and made $41. It was one of the best experiences of my life."

This is clearly the first time he's ever discussed break-dancing in a membership meeting.

I take him through the story of my friend Myron and me convincing my sister to drive across a few state lines to break-dance and make some money. I do it in under three minutes. Then I tell him I've only eaten fruit until noon for twenty-seven years, I have the same friends from elementary school, I used to manage my favorite music group of all time, Run-DMC, I ran 100 miles, I lived with a Navy SEAL for thirty-one days, and I just got back from a two-week stint at a monastery with monks. Monks who've lived there for fifty years.

"Oh," I say. "And I have a wife, four kids, and a lot of gratitude for life."

Ted's mouth is open. He has perfect teeth; they must have cost his parents a fortune.

"Did you say you lived with a Navy SEAL?"

"Yeah, and wrote a book about it."

"And you've just come back from living at a monastery?"

"Yeah. The monks I stayed with breed German shepherds and train dogs."

"German shepherds?"

"Oh, and the nuns make cheesecake."

"They make cheesecake?"

"Delicious. I'll have them send you one if you like. You like cheesecake?"

"Um, not really, but whatever possessed you to go live at a monastery?"

"Have you ever read the book *The Monk Who Sold His Ferrari* by Robin Sharma? It's the story of a lawyer who loses everything and finds himself."

"I haven't read it, but is that why you went there? To find yourself?"

"No, I went there to find out how to live my life in a more meaningful way."

"Did you?"

"What I found was that I already knew how to live my life in a meaningful way. It's like the wiring had been put in place the entire time. The monks just showed me where the ON switch was. Don't get me wrong, we're not all wired to be monks. I went there to get a piece of the monks. It's like those DNA kits they can send to your home to find your nationalities. Except this is different; I wanted to make monk 10 percent of my DNA, not 100 percent."

I spend the next fifteen minutes telling him about my experience. And then I mention I'm writing a book about it. He's fascinated. He tells me he's always romanticized about taking some sort of spiritual sabbatical, but he just hasn't been able to find the time. He keeps firing questions at me, and I hit them right back to him.

"This is why I think life résumés are more important," I

say. "Think about it, if you're at work, who do you want to sit next to at the lunch table—the guy who volunteers at a prison on the weekends and has a painting studio in his house OR the guy who's spent his whole life crunching numbers and analyzing the economy?"

"Prison painter?"

"I agree. And I also believe networking has become shallow," I say. "Everyone is so concerned with connecting on social media, adding followers, collecting business cards, and shaking as many hands as they can at a cocktail party. But how strong is that network when you really don't know the people? Sure, coffee is great, but I still think you need to go deeper. That's why experiences are so important, especially experiences you do with others. Right now I can call and count on people who I have deep connections with, not because I bought them a bagel and followed up with a thank-you email. It's because I have true connections, moments if you will, and experiences that will last a lifetime. If you ever climb Mount Washington with someone, they'll be your friend for life. An experience is like making a deposit in the bank. We can draw on it at any time."

Ted stands up to shake my hand.

"I really hope you consider our club. We'd love to have you."

I fight the urge to tell him, "Thanks, but no thanks."

What's that old line by Groucho Marx? I'd never join a club that'd have me as a member?

Something like that.

As I walk through the lobby to the parking lot, my

thoughts are clear. If you want to live like a monk, good for you, but do it at a monastery. If you want to live life in the outside world, live it with urgency, and build your life résumé.

Part of my "why" as it relates to the monastery was to add to my life résumé. It's another experience, another adventure, another thing I can look back on and be proud of as I get older. I'm a believer in having a bucket list. Bucket lists are great! Meeting Mick Jagger is on mine. But I'm a MUCH bigger believer in dropping the "b" in bucket, adding an "f" to create a "fuck-it list." The fuck-it list is a collection of things you always wanted to do, but maybe were too scared, felt the timing wasn't right, or maybe you believed you didn't have enough experience. They are the things that require some risk, some fear, and may result in failure. BUT those are the things that make you feel most alive.

    After many days of edits and reading the manuscript over and over again, I finally open up my computer and attach the document in an email to my editor. I click send. The email box vanishes from my screen. I grab my pen and walk over to my fuck-it list and cross off number 33.

33. ~~Living with monks at a monastery~~
34. Ride a bike across the country
35. Learn sign language
36. Black belt in Krav Maga
37. Write a screenplay
38.

A Final Thought

Here's what I want everyone who finished reading this book to do. Go to www.jesseitzler.com/liferesume and sign your name and list the one thing you're going to go out and do with urgency that you've been wanting to do but haven't found the right time. An experience that is out of your comfort zone and perhaps scary. And once a month for an entire year after my book publishes I'm going to pick one person at random and compensate their adventure if they supply a proof of purchase. And the list has already started...

1. Turney Duff—I'm going to take a stand-up comedy class
2. Lisa Leshne—Heli-Skiing
3. Kate Hartson—Take a fencing class
4. Brian McDonald—I'm going to sign up for a trapeze class
5. Sara Blakely—I want to run a half marathon
6. Lazer Itzler—I'm going to camp out on Mount Washington in the winter
7. Marq Brown—I'm going to run the Boston Marathon
8.
9.
10.

AFTERWORD

Post-Monastery Update to the Trade Edition

Stay in the Game

*"Be true to the game, because the game will be true
to you. If you try to shortcut the game, then the game
will shortcut you. If you put forth the effort, good
things will be bestowed upon you. That's truly about
the game, and in some ways that's about life too."*
— MICHAEL JORDAN

I didn't move to a monastery to become a monk. That wasn't
my plan. I intended to learn how to better navigate the ever-
chaotic buzzing world we live in and possibly pick up secrets.
And I consider my trip a success. Like many of us, I needed
a digital detox. What I discovered was that we'd all be a little
happier, have more freedom, and accomplish more if we tap
into the monks' lifestyle at least a little bit, like 10 percent.

The monks enlightened me on the beauty and benefits of
monotasking. They helped shape my perspective on time and
taught me how to avoid unnecessary distractions. My definition of happiness changed, and my thought process improved.
And for that, I'll be forever grateful.

But months after my sabbatical, the magic monk dust
starts to settle. I begin feeling a pull. At first, it's like a faint
whisper from my subconscious. It's saying, *Do more.* The

voice becomes louder and louder until it's screaming—*DO MORE!* It's an itch I must scratch. I want—no, *need* to do more. **I keep telling myself that this is the only shot I have at life, and I don't want to look back when I'm seventy-five and say I was the 80 percent version of myself.** None of us want to be the 80 percent version of ourselves.

Soon I'm drawn into an almost manic pace. That's just who I am, and it makes me happy. But now I realize that the key is to pursue it—whatever *it* is—which requires holding on to 10 percent of the monks' wisdom. To stay active, I load my schedule with speaking gigs. And as I share my story with more and more people, it creates a new lane for me.

I'm interacting with folks from all over the country who desire to be pushed to their limits and improve the quality of their lives, and some who just want to get off the couch. I love it. It's like fuel to me. I'm motivated to motivate others. And from this experience, my Build Your Life Resume course is born. I start coaching individuals and groups on how to achieve goals, create memories, and do more.

While I continually develop the course, I look for something else—something more.

At this stage of my life, I try to seek business opportunities that are low in aggravation and high in reward. When I was younger, I could handle unnecessary hassle if the potential payoff was significant, but now if something comes with the extra baggage, it's a pass. (I even use this rule when traveling—I always carry my own bag.) So I start thinking: *How can I put an event together that's something I love, something I'm good at (or at least can get good at), while also having a purpose?*

One night my wheels are turning when I go to pick up Lazer from football practice. My son comes running over to me and jumps into my arms. That's when I see his coach lacing up his running sneakers. His name is Marc, and he's probably ten years younger than me and looks every bit of it. When he starts stretching, it occurs to me he's running home after practice—I like it. So I strike up a conversation, and we instantly click. And within a few minutes, we discover our shared passion for endurance events.

"We should keep a dialogue going," I say. "Maybe we can do an event together one day."

As I begin thinking, I establish specific criteria of what kind of business model I'd want to do. I start telling myself the event needs to be fun and worthwhile. It needs to be unique, challenging, something I'm excited about, with a major cool factor. When people hear about it, it should raise eyebrows, cock heads, and crack smiles. I've always been a fan of the summer camp model—whoever invented that is a genius. Work eight weeks, and then you're off for the rest of the year? Brilliant. Work fewer weeks, but still get an excellent return. Once I feel like I'm traveling down the right path, I continue to develop it.

Two days later, I pick Lazer up from practice and see Marc lacing his shoes again.

"Hey, Marc," I say. "Wouldn't it be cool to hike to the top of Mount Everest?"

"Um, yeah," he says. "And expensive."

"We should do it. Let's plan an event around climbing Everest."

"Okay," he says. "But that's not realistic."

"I bet a lot of folks want to know if they have what it takes to climb Everest."

"Um...We live in Atlanta?"

"Exactly!"

"I'm not following."

"What if there's another way?"

✥✥✥✥✥

Over the next few months, we start brainstorming. Once we think we know what the target is we rent Stratton Mountain, a ski resort in Vermont, for a weekend in October, and we decide to call the event 29029. Our idea is unique: a three-day retreat combined with an endurance event. But it's the challenge that's the real hook. All participants will attempt to hike up the mountain and take the gondola back down. They'll repeat it seventeen times, which is the vertical equivalent of climbing Mount Everest (29,029 feet).

Marc and I decide to make the event open to two hundred people; we want to keep it friendly and have a community feel. The plan is to have everyone eat meals together, listen to speakers together, and tackle the mountain together. As we make all of the necessary arrangements, we continue building out the core idea. We want to create a community of like-minded people and connect them through endurance challenges while providing a self-discovery experience. Our formula is the unknown of being able to complete the challenge + a connection to the outdoors and nature + unri-valed camaraderie = a worthy addition to your life résumé.

I believe memories that pay dividends are the most valu-able kind. I know firsthand, like living on the monastery, that an attempted challenge enhances all areas of my life: busi-ness, parenting, relationship, and physical fitness. When I test myself so intensely, I can bring that same level of persever-ance and struggle into any future endeavor. We can evolve into our best selves. And I think 29029 will be precisely that.

✿✿✿✿✿

October rolls around, and the first 29029 kicks off. We've created a village, hired bands, set up a bonfire pit, and sched-uled inspirational speakers. Food trucks are parked in the parking lot, sports drinks and adult beverages are on tap, and high-end tents are set up for the sleeping quarters. It's like Burning Man meets Ironman. All participants have three days to reach their Everest. Over the last month, I've taken a few trial runs, and it's steep. So my guess is that Grizzly Adams could do it in twenty-five minutes, but if you're really in shape, maybe forty-five minutes, and if you're in decent shape it'll likely take an hour for each hike up.

By Friday afternoon, everyone's arrived. The sun is shin-ing, and it's almost go time. We gather at the starting area. I introduce myself and thank everyone for coming. Then I provide a blueprint as best I can. I tell them this is going to be fun, hard, and—well, I don't really know what else to expect, so that makes it even more exciting. After explaining the safety measures we've taken, I look out over the crowd. I see excited and fearful eyes and adrenaline pumping in the people ready to do this. So screw it—let's do this!

We're off... Everyone is allowed to climb into the night, but the gondola closes at 5:00 p.m. So if you want to keep going, you can, but it'll require using headlamps and maybe some warmer clothes. If you get to the top after closing time, we have SUVs making trips up and down the mountain. I plan to knock out as many as I can without stopping. I've been training, I'm in good shape, and the terrain isn't affecting me. I feel good.

I'm hiking up the mountain one trip at a time. The views are spectacular. And on my fifth or sixth trip, I suddenly start thinking about the guys at the monastery. They'd love this event. The joy on their faces when we hiked up that hill—I mean road—is seared into my brain forever. And then I start remembering the driveway—ah yes, the driveway. I walked up and down that thing so many times I could schematic the shit out of it; I could tell you where every bump, pothole, and crack was. As I keep going it's like the monks are with me. I keep hiking.

The 29029 epiphany didn't happen while I was at the monastery, but maybe 10 percent of the idea was born up there. I remember exactly where I was on the driveway when I recalled my Remember Tomorrow mantra. It saved me. Those walks helped me process everything I was learning and exposed to, and they gave me time to think and absorb.

On my eighth trip up Stratton Mountain, I start feeling it. My muscles burn, and a rash forms on my legs. Up ahead I see my friend Mike, one of my boys I grew up with in Roslyn. He's lumbering. I think he's one lap behind me, so he's on his seventh trip. When I catch him, I ask how he's doing. No words come out of his mouth, but I'm fairly fluent in facial expressions, and I interpret his as *not well, dude, not well at all.*

"I hear you," I say, even though he didn't say anything. He finally grunts and then tells me he's had fun, but this is it, this is his last one. He explains that with the way he feels right now, he knows he won't be able to complete it. And I know what he's doing because I used to do it. He's projecting. Mike is calculating the pain based on how he feels right now. And there's no way he can endure another ten hours of it.

I feel the same way. It's cold, I'm sore, and it'd be so easy to quit. My brain tries to convince me I'll feel like this forever. Billy the Bully likes to lie, but the truth is that at some point, this event will be over. And once you quit anything, you're done, but if you stay in the game, anything can happen.

"Just one more hike up," I say on our way back down. "And then we'll reassess."

"Okay, man," he says. "I just need to go to the bathroom."

Mike and I both know he's done and that's okay. I've got a job to do, and that's called hike number nine. And then a funny thing happens: I feel better. Call it magic, luck, or second wind. I don't care what you call it; it's all the same. It's just how I felt a week in at the monastery and at many other moments in my life when things looked bleak. We think it'll never get better and believe in our core that we're stuck where we are forever. And then there's a metaphorical shift, and the incline becomes a decline.

I can do this. Trip ten, eleven, twelve, thirteen, fourteen, fifteen, and sixteen up the mountain. Not all easy, but

I'm confident and almost taste the gratification. It's time for my last hike. For the entire event I've been wearing a white bib along with everyone else, but on the last hike, the hikers switch to a red Final Ascent bib along with a 29029 flag to bring to the top. I start my last hike up...

I'm solo and running on pure adrenaline. I feel stronger with each step—higher and higher. I pass the vaunted 7 POLES REMAINING sign, and then 6 POLES REMAINING, and then 5 POLES REMAINING, and on and on. I keep moving. Eventually, I hear music in the distance and see the finish line. Each stride I take is closer to my goal. And with one final step, I cross that line. It feels great. Alone, looking at the valley below, I smile. This is nice. And like any great spiritual journey, this one ends on a mountaintop.

The Wall of Fear

"If you're scared to take chances, you'll never have the answers.
I could tell the future of a dude by how his stance is."

—NAS

November 2018 to February 2019

Shit! I click the internet access button again on my laptop for the fifteenth time. And for the fifteenth time it won't connect. Not good—I have an online Build Your Life Resume Q&A session starting in six minutes with 650 eager clients waiting for me. It's the coaching course I offer. But right now I need a Wi-Fi coach. I still can't connect.

Sara and I moved into our new home this past summer, and the kinks haven't been worked out yet—like the temperamental internet connection in my office. It worked yesterday, but not the day before. I click the button again. I get nothing. I've got four minutes. Time to call an audible.

I yank the cords and hold my laptop like I'm delivering a pizza to your table. Then I grab my notes and folders with my other hand and race out of my office. Turney is walking down the stairs as I'm running up. When he sees me, he stands in a frozen appraisal, observing like a birdwatcher who spotted an orange-bellied parrot—the rarest of birds. He can't figure out what I'm doing. But I don't have time to talk because I only have three minutes left.

"DoyouknowhowtoconnecttomyWi-Fi," I say whizzing past him.

"What?"

"Never mind," I say from the top of the stairs.

In my bedroom I hook up the computer and get online exactly when the call starts.

I did it.

The Build Your Life Resume course is a coaching program I created. It focuses on helping people in three main buckets of their lives: business, mindset, and wellness. I started it after years of seeing other coaching programs charge exorbitant amounts of money and being taught by people who haven't walked the walk. They're offered by marketers, not coaches. My mission is to offer a course that yields lifelong results—and one of the best ways to get results is by personally connecting to the people taking the course (thank you, bedroom Wi-Fi gods).

My call goes smoothly and without any technical difficulties. I enjoy doing Q&As because I never know what's coming. It's like a baseball player standing in the batter's box waiting for the next pitch. Is the pitcher going to throw a fastball, a changeup, or perhaps a nasty curve? I never know, but I love taking a swing at it. And I believe I've had enough at-bats that I can hit almost any pitch, even if it's in the dirt.

Near the end of my call, a woman tells me she just finished reading *Living with the Monks*, and she wants to know how it changed me. I think about it for a moment. Did it change me? Well, it's not like I wake up and meditate and pray every morning. So I haven't turned into a monk. And my hair did grow back, so...

"I wouldn't say it changed me per se," I say. "It's provided me with insight into one of my character defects, like trying to do too much too fast. So the experience has helped slow me down when I need to. Plus it's another thing on the résumé. I can access my monk experience at any time. It's come in handy a few times during stressful situations. I went to the monks because I wanted to speed up my spiritual process. As an entrepreneur **I know that one of the most important things you can do is speed up the process. I'm constantly asking myself how can I get to point B the fastest.**"

As for spirituality, I didn't want to listen to fifty podcasts or read a ton of books about monk-ism. I'm a slow reader. So I accelerated the process by going to New Skete. I know what I did was a fifteen-day investment, which a lot of people can't do, but it was an immersive experience that was invaluable. I can't put a price on that. **I've realized that lasting change takes time**—I learned that from the monks. Often people sign up for this conference or that retreat; they pay $800 for the weekend and believe they're going to get immediate results. But it doesn't work that way. Whatever journey you're on, it usually takes quite some time to get there.

And since I left the monastery **I've found myself asking myself one specific question that drills right down to the heart of my effort—a monk's effort. I posted it on Instagram a little while ago: Ask yourself, would you recommend yourself as a _____? Would you recommend yourself as a CEO, employee, husband,**

friend, or whatever? And if the answer is no, then ask yourself, why not? It's amazing how that one simple self-reflection can be the perfect scorecard around your effort.

Shortly after wrapping up the Q&A, I go looking for Turney. But I can't find him anywhere. I search the whole house. So I head to the kitchen and I'm three spoonfuls into my smoothie bowl when he lumbers into the kitchen.

"Where were you?"

"Oh," he says. "I was sitting on the toilet—thinking."

"Nice. Ready to work?"

Turney came down to Atlanta for a few days to work on a new idea I have. I want to do a documentary-type thing targeting the cereal industry. I'm not exactly sure what it is yet, but I'd like to disrupt the whole industry. I've always been intrigued and passionate about the deceptive advertising behind cereal. Big companies overstate the nutritional benefits and market what is essentially sugar and processed food to children. I'm still thinking through the details of the project in my head, but the working title is #CerealKillers. The two of us are working with my friend Def Jef and my college buddy Jon. We're trying to develop it and figure out what it is.

After a few hours of brainstorming my phone rings. The name on the screen: Grant Cardone.

Grant is something of a sales guru, bestselling author, renowned motivational speaker, and a savvy investor who hosts conferences, workshops, and events. And he has a massively loyal following. About a year ago Grant asked Sara and me to speak at one of his events in Miami. Sara crushed it, but it wasn't one of my best outings. They asked me to speak for thirty minutes, which is like the worst time allotment for me. Thirty minutes is no man's land.

My sweet spot is under twenty minutes or forty plus. So when I was faced with thirty I decided todelivermyusualfortyminutetalkanddoitreallyreallyfastandsayeverythingIwantedinthirtyminutes.

It was received okay, but I know I could have done better.

"Hey, Grant," I say into my phone.

After a quick catch-up, Grant tells me he's doing another conference in Miami in early February and he'd like me and Sara to speak again. I'm flattered, but given our schedules, I'm not sure if it'll sync up. So I tell him I'll have to get back to him.

"We're expecting thirty-five thousand people," he says.

He must mean thirty-five hundred, so I give him a chance to correct himself ... Nothing comes during the pause in our conversation. He's waiting for me to respond.

"Thirty-five thousand?"

"Yup."

"Tony Robbins doesn't get thirty-five thousand. That's ridiculous. Who else is speaking?"

"I'm not sure," he says. "I haven't set the lineup yet."

That night I talk it over with Sara. We decide we're going do it. Why not? But there's no way he's putting thirty-five thousand butts in the seats. How is that even possible? If he gets 10 percent of that number it'll be a good-sized audience. The next morning I call Grant and tell him we are in, and he tells me they're giving me an hour on stage. *Great*, I think. *I can do an hour.* But he never tells me what to talk about or even asks what I'm talking about—it's like free swim at the pool. The only direction I get is that I'll be on the stage for sixty minutes. Got it.

I've got two months to prepare. There's *no way* I'm going to wait until the last minute for this. It's too big of an opportunity. I want to knock it out of the park. And then the holidays happen. As we get closer to the event Grant gives periodic updates: We're at 18k, 21k, 24k. The updates are like watching a Jerry Lewis telethon—the numbers keep rising. And then he relays to me: 27k, 33k, and then finally we're sold out at 35k. Okay, now I'm nervous.

Instead of practicing, I begin building what I call the wall of fear in my head. I don't envision a standing ovation or extended applause. Nope, nothing like that. I envision pure failure. What if I forget my lines? What if people can't hear me and they leave in the middle of it? What if I bomb? With each negative thought, the wall of fear gets higher and higher.

I'm flipping out—thirty-five thousand people.

I believe with 100 percent certainty that everyone in their lifetime will likely build a giant wall of fear—many of them, in fact. And each of us is the architect, designer, and builder of that wall. The wall is created by our own negative thoughts. We stack bricks of fear in front of us. And the more we pile up those thoughts, the higher the wall becomes.

We have two choices as we approach that wall: we can turn around and get the hell out of there, or we can go right through that motherfucker. On the other side of that wall— if we can get over it—lies a euphoric high. That's where the reward is. The question is, **Are you going to let that wall of fear keep you away from where you want to go, or are you going to figure out how to get to the other side of it?**

A couple of weeks later I'm stressing and talking with Def Jef.

"Everything is going to be fine. You've got enough reps," he says. "Trust it."

He's right. I've done speaking events hundreds of times. I've put the work in. And it's happening. I'm going on at 1:20 p.m. on Friday—no matter what—and I'll be done by 2:30 p.m. It's going to be over in one hour and life will still go on. I realize I need to break through my wall of fear. I can't stop the clock. And as long as I have an hour, I may as well nail it.

I start taking a wrecking ball to the wall of fear.

I considered changing my talk, reworking it, rewriting it, but nah, I'm just going to trust it. So Sara and I fly to Miami on Thursday. It's a three-day conference. We check into the hotel and hit a sushi restaurant that night. It's like a wannabe Nobu. We get seated and a few attendees come over and introduce themselves. They want to take pictures and shoot the shit. It's firing me up. I'm turning the fear into enthusiasm. **That's a trick I always try to tell people to use: flip your fear to enthusiasm.**

I wake up the next morning and go for a long run. It's mostly excitement running through my bloodstream, but fear still lingers. After a quick shower I head over to the venue—Marlins Park. Wow! And the lineup is great—Sara, Steve Harvey, John Maxwell, Bethenny Frankel, Daymond John, Tai Lopez, and Ryan Deiss, to name a few. The nerves start pumping again.

I try to calm myself down in the green room. I realize sitting still is making it worse. I need to walk around. I get up and head over to the back of the stage and then look out to the sea of people. It feels like I'm at Shea Stadium getting ready to throw out the first pitch on opening day.

Thirty-five thousand people looks like thirty-five thousand people—wow.

I go back to the green room and find a corner for some privacy. I close my eyes and take a few deep breaths. I can do this. Breathe in. Breathe out. Breathe in. Breathe out. Breathe in. Breathe out. Okay, how would a monk advise me to talk to thirty-five thousand people? The answer immediately hits me: he wouldn't. A monk would tell me I'm talking to one person thirty-five thousand times. $1 \times 35{,}000$. That's some core monk shit right there. Instantly I feel ready.

Let's do this. I hit the stage...

In some ways I feel like I'm the warm-up band coming on before the main act. Steve Harvey and my wife are after me. I know most people in the audience won't be familiar with me, which is cool, but it may be a disadvantage. So I have to commit the first part of my speech to building credibility. No one is going to respond to what I say unless they believe I know what I'm saying. It's no different than in business: **people buy into the people more than they do the products**.

I tell my story, beat by beat. I speak slower than normal because the sound system in such a large venue creates a tiny echo, and slowing down actually helps me. I hit my marks with the brownie story, getting a record deal, running one hundred miles, Marquis Jet, and speeding up the process. And with every story I provide the main takeaway. I feel good. It feels good.

I did it. Then after the Q&A with Grant and pitching my Build Your Life Resume course, I walk off the stage. I can't stop smiling. As I look back on the journey I see a hole in the middle of the big wall of fear with my silhouette running right through it.

Acknowledgments

The monks of New Skete reminded me of the importance of having a strong community. With its support we can exceed our wildest expectations. I would like to take a moment to thank my community and tribe on this project: Turney Duff, Lisa Leshne, Jennifer Kish, Marc Adelman, Kenny Reisman, Marq Brown, Jef Fortson, Jon Cornick, Marc Hodulich, Brian McDonald, Kate Hartson, Rolf Zettersten, all those at Center Street Books, and DeeDee Debartlo. I'm so grateful for your time and efforts. I also want to thank Josh the Cook for all the amazing meals (and newspapers) and Lenny the Intern for sparing me. You kept me on my toes, Lenny, and I'm glad we became "almost" friends!

A heartfelt thank-you to the remarkable nuns of New Skete—Sister Patricia, Sister Cecilia, and Sister Rebecca. I'm so grateful for how you accepted me into your monastery, for your wisdom, and for the delicious cheesecake.

Obviously this book would not have been possible without the welcoming love and support of the monks of New Skete. A huge spiritual shout-out to Brother Thomas, Brother Christopher, Brother Stavros, Brother Mark, Brother John, Brother Luke, Brother Peter, Brother Gregory, Brother Ambrose. Your warmth and hospitality went above and beyond what was expected. Thanks for making me feel so at home and thanks for all the bananas (sorry about those Clif Bars).

Lastly, I want to thank my incredibly loving and encouraging wife, Sara, for holding down the fort while I was gone. Thanks for letting me use some of my 36,000 free hours on this adventure and letting me fill my plate with what I love to do. I told her that this trip would allow me to be more "present" in our relationship going forward. I hope I was right. I'm so lucky to have you. And thank you for all of your support on my quest to building my life résumé.

#WhatsNext

Jesse

About the Author

Jesse Itzler only eats fruit until noon, loves Run D.M.C., and enjoys living life "out of the box"—actually he doesn't even have a box. He co-founded Marquis Jet, the world's largest prepaid private jet card company in 2001, which he and his partner sold to Berkshire Hathaway/NetJets. He then helped pioneer the coconut water craze with Zico coconut water, which he and his partners sold to The Coco-Cola Company in 2013. He is a former rapper on MTV, and he produced both the NBA's Emmy Award-winning "I Love This Game" music campaign and the popular New York Knicks anthem "Go NY Go." In 2016 he authored *Living with a SEAL* which went on to be a *New York Times* bestseller. When he is not running ultramarathons or being a dad to his four kids, Jesse can be found at the NBA's Atlanta Hawks games, where he is an owner of the team. He is married to Spanx founder Sara Blakely, and the couple and their four children live in Atlanta, Georgia.